BLOODY BUNA

Bloody Buna

The campaign that halted the Japanese invasion
of Australia

LIDA MAYO

NEW ENGLISH LIBRARY
TIMES MIRROR

To Charles V. P. von Luttichau

First published in the USA by Doubleday Company. Inc
First published in Great Britain by David & Charles in 1975
© 1974 by Doubleday Company, Inc

*

FIRST NEL PAPERBACK EDITION JUNE 1977

*

NEL Books are published by
New English Library Limited from Barnard's Inn, Holborn, London EC1N 2JR
Made and printed in Great Britain by Hunt Barnard Printing Ltd., Aylesbury, Bucks.

45003192 6

Contents

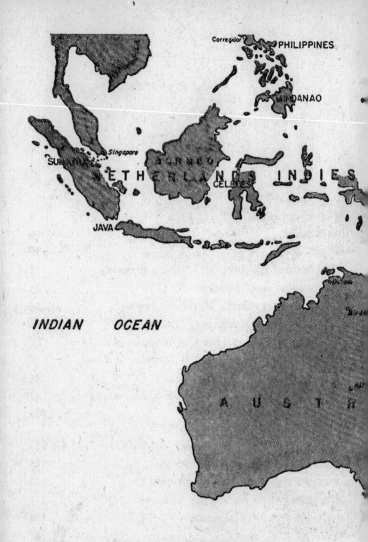

THE SOUTHWEST PACIFIC

0   800 MILES

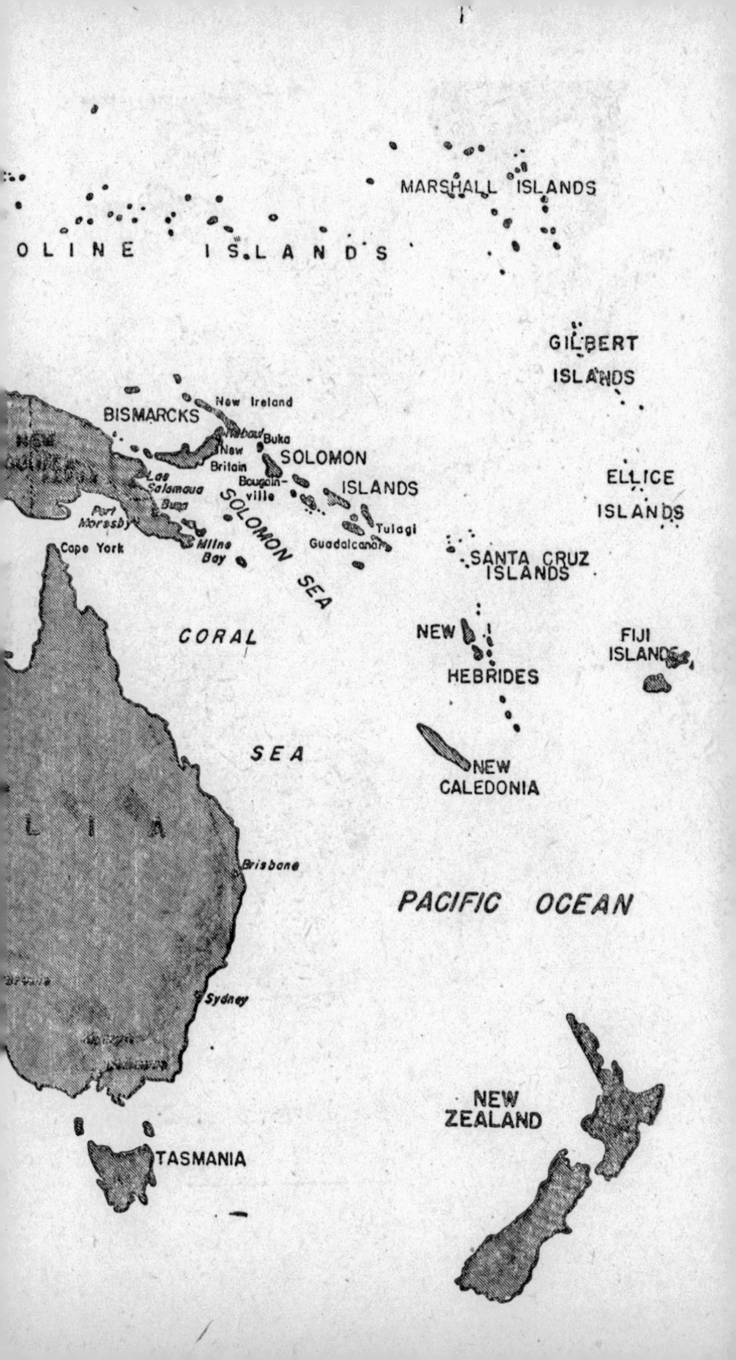
MARSHALL ISLANDS
OLINE ISLANDS
GILBERT
ISLANDS
New Ireland
BISMARCKS
Rabaul
Buka
New
Britain
SOLOMON
ISLANDS
Salamaua
Buna
Port
Moresby
Bougainville
SOLOMON SEA
Tulagi
Guadalcanal
Milne
Bay
Cape York
ELLICE
ISLANDS
SANTA CRUZ
ISLANDS
CORAL
SEA
NEW
HEBRIDES
FIJI
ISLANDS
NEW
CALEDONIA
Brisbane
PACIFIC OCEAN
Sydney
NEW
ZEALAND
TASMANIA

Acknowledgments

I owe a great debt of gratitude to Hanson W. Baldwin for the loan of personal papers and, most of all, for a discerning critique of the entire manuscript. If errors remain (as Mr Baldwin wrote in his *Battles Lost and Won*, published by Harper & Row in 1966, 'the writing of military history is an inexact art'), they are mine alone. Grateful acknowledgment is due John Toland for the loan of material he gathered in preparing *The Rising Sun* (Random House: 1970). The late Major General Edwin F. Harding lent me excerpts from his diary; Colonel Maxwell Emerson and Colonel John E. Harbert wrote me at length of their experiences at Buna.

My former colleagues at the U.S. Army's Office of the Chief of Military History have been most helpful, notably Charles V. P. von Luttichau, Mary Ann Bacon, Billy C. Mossman, Joseph R. Friedman, Charles B. MacDonald, Detmar Finke, Martin Blumenson, and Edna Salsbury.

On a research visit to Australia and New Guinea in November 1967 I was given the utmost assistance by the staff of the Australian War Memorial in Canberra, especially A. J. Sweeting, Mary E. Gilchrist, Mike Cartner, and Bruce Harding. Gavin Long in Canberra, Osmar White in Melbourne, and H. Leslie Williams in New Guinea gave generously of their time in interviews. The latter, who was District Officer in Popondetta, made it possible for me to visit Gona and Buna.

For aid on illustrations I wish to thank the Australian War Memorial and the U.S. Army Audio-Visual Agency; also, Lucy Lazarou, the Reverend E. W. M. Kelly, and Mrs S. A. Jenkinson. The maps were prepared by Arthur S. Hardyman with skill and understanding.

L.M.

List of Maps

Author's Note

The battle for Buna in New Guinea, won by General Douglas MacArthur in January 1943 – the Allies' first major land victory over the Japanese in World War II, began in July 1942, but for many months had little coverage in the American press, mainly because of tight censorship at MacArthur's headquarters. Guadalcanal received the headlines. Not until late in 1942 did Americans become fully aware of the bitterness of the struggle for Buna, summed up in *Time* magazine on December 28, 1942: 'Nowhere in the world today are American soldiers engaged in fighting so desperate, so merciless, so bitter, or so bloody.'

Bloody Buna has been written with the help of two official histories: Samuel Milner's *Victory in Papua* (Office of the Chief of Military History, Department of the Army, series *U.S. Army in World War II:* 1957) and Dudley McCarthy's *South-west Pacific – First Year: Kokoda to Wau* (Australian War Memorial, series *Australia in the War of 1939–1945:* 1959). One or the other can be assumed to be the basis of the narrative, unless another source is cited.

When Milner began his research a few years after the war, he collected firsthand accounts of the battle by interviews, correspondence, and the loan of private papers (see *Victory in Papua*, pp. 381–82). Later, the draft of his manuscript was sent to important participants for review and comment. These comments, along with Milner's notes on interviews, his correspondence, and his copies of private papers, are deposited in the Washington National Records Center. They are cited in *Bloody Buna* as Milner File.

"I CAME THROUGH, AND
I SHALL RETURN"

Since dawn on Saturday, March 21, 1942, a crisp, clear, blue-and-gold autumn day in southern Australia, the people of Melbourne had been converging on Spencer Street Railway Station to welcome General Douglas MacArthur, jamming the street outside the brownstone Victorian station, packing the roofs of neighboring buildings, pushing, jostling, in surges of excitement.

Excitement had been growing since Tuesday, when the radio broke the news of MacArthur's escape from the Philippines. In the darkness of night the general and his party, which included his wife and child, had been smuggled out of Corregidor in four torpedo boats. Slipping through the Japanese Navy's cordon, the little boats managed to land their passengers on Mindanao in the southern Philippines. There the general's party was picked up by bombers and flown to an airfield near Darwin on the northern coast of Australia.

The day he stepped on Australian soil, General MacArthur made a statement to the press: 'The President of the United States ordered me to break through the Japanese lines and proceed from Corregidor to Australia for the purpose, as I understand it, of organizing the American offensive against Japan. A primary purpose of this is the relief of the Philippines.' Here he paused, and on his final words laid great emphasis: *'I came through, and I shall return.'*

The Australians hailed him as a savior. Rumors quickly spread that a million Americans were on their way across the Pacific to rescue Australia.

For three months the great arc of protecting islands on her north had been crumbling under the attack launched by the Japanese in December 1941. After the capture in late January 1942 of Rabaul in the Bismarcks on the eastern end of the arc and the fall of Singapore in mid-February at the western end, many Australians felt that invasion of the mainland could be expected at any time. On February 19, Darwin was bombed, the first attack in the nation's history. When the news reached the southeastern coast, where most of the population was concentrated, barbed wire was strung around the beaches at Sydney and Melbourne, and a brownout was imposed.

In the past two weeks the lights had gone out entirely in the southeastern cities. On March 8 the Japanese invaded New Guinea, the great primitive, dragon-shaped island that appears on the map to be about to perch on a peninsula jutting up from Australia's northeastern coast. They captured two villages on the lower back of the dragon, Lae and Salamaua, villages only 400 miles by air from Cape York on the tip of the Australian peninsula. Tokyo Radio indeed announced a landing at Cape York; this was discounted as propaganda, but it was disquieting. On the very morning of MacArthur's arrival in Melbourne, one of the city's newspapers carried the headline: AIR SUPREMACY MAY SAVE AUSTRALIA: WOULD OFFSET JAP LANDINGS.

At 10 o'clock General MacArthur stepped down from his train, and a great cheer went up; people surged against the iron fence around the station platform and had to be beaten back by black-helmeted policemen. When he came into view, the Australians went wild. He wore no insignia on his belted cotton jacket, his only sign of rank his high-peaked cap embroidered in gold, but there was no mistaking MacArthur. Tall and erect, he did not look his sixty-two years; there was no trace of gray in his black hair. With great presence and a natural air of command, he walked across the platform in all 'his inimitable strolling magnificence'. In his left hand he carried a cane, with his right he waved to the crowd, and his handsome aquiline face broke into a smile.

Behind the confident bearing, the smile, was a man deeply shaken and dismayed.

He had left Corregidor believing that he had been ordered out to take command of a huge force being assembled in

14

Australia for the relief of the Philippines. As soon as he landed at Darwin, he asked an American officer at the airfield how many American troops were in Australia. The officer replied, 'As far as I know, sir, there are very few troops here.' MacArthur stared; walking away, he remarked, 'Surely he is wrong.'

Two commercial airliners were waiting to take his party to Melbourne, 2,000 miles to the south. General MacArthur announced that he wished to travel by train. Members of his party were not surprised, because they knew he suffered from airsickness and never flew if he could help it; but the Australians were disconcerted. They told him that the only railway line out of Darwin stopped at Birdum, 300 miles to the south, and that from Birdum a dusty rutted road was the only means of traveling more than 600 miles to Alice Springs, the northern terminus of the Central Australian Railway. This the general found hard to believe; maps had to be produced to convince him. At last he agreed to fly as far as Alice Springs, but no farther.

Landing at Alice Springs, a hot, dreary little town almost exactly in the center of Australia, MacArthur, sending his Deputy Chief of Staff, Brigadier General Richard J. Marshall, ahead by air to Melbourne, took the primitive little narrow-gauge train whose speed was not much more than 20 miles an hour. It took three days to travel the 800 miles to Terowie, the junction with the broad-gauge line to Melbourne. Rattling and jouncing through the desert hinterland, MacArthur discussed with his staff the prospects for a quick return to the Philippines. The logical jump-off point was Darwin; but the impossibility of getting troops and supplies overland to Darwin was now all too apparent, even if, as MacArthur continued to believe, a large American force had been landed at Sydney or Melbourne.

At Terowie a comfortable private car was waiting. Aboard was General Marshall with information that shattered MacArthur's hopes. Only about 25,000 American troops were in Australia, and these were mainly air, antiaircraft, or engineer units; moreover, American aircraft, on which the Australians largely depended, had incurred heavy losses in repelling attacks on Darwin. As for Australian forces, the bulk of the regular army was in the Middle East; one division and one brigade had been ordered home, but all had not yet arrived. Not only were there no troops for a return to the Philippines, there were not even enough to defend Australia.

All that night, as the train traveled toward Melbourne, MacArthur paced the corridor of his car in the bitter realization, as he recalled later, that he had been 'moved into an area and into a sector which was almost as menaced as the Philippines'. His problem was no longer 'how to go back to the Philippines – that army was doomed. It was how to defend this great country from being doomed, too.'

His bitterness was discernible in the statement he prepared for the press next morning as the train neared Melbourne. Success, he pointed out, depended on the amount of manpower and matériel the Australian and American governments would give him: 'No general can make something of nothing.'

In the official welcoming party on the station platform at Melbourne was Lieutenant General George H. Brett, the tough, stocky air officer who until MacArthur's arrival had been in command of all the American forces in Australia. Brett thought that MacArthur, close up, looked weary and drawn. After giving out his statement, he walked to his waiting car, curtly refusing Brett's offer to accompany him, and was driven to the Menzies Hotel, an old-fashioned hotel with sumptuous plush hangings and a dimly lit interior. An entire floor had been reserved for MacArthur and his party, and they were given their own telephone exchange, call designation (at their request), 'Bataan'.

The officers who had accompanied General MacArthur from the Philippines and who were to form the nucleus of his staff in Australia were nicknamed by American war correspondents 'the Bataan gang'. Of these, the closest to MacArthur was his Chief of Staff, Major General Richard K. Sutherland, whom he had – in the dark days in the Philippines – recommended as his successor in the event of his death. Sutherland continued to have MacArthur's unswerving confidence and time after time was to serve as his 'eyes and ears'. A handsome man with a Roman profile, son of a justice of the Supreme Court, he was described by a fellow member of the Bataan gang as a 'hard man' who inspired respect rather than affection; but he would 'sometimes break the mask of hardness with a sardonic smile and curious flashes of humor'.

Along with the amenities at the Menzies Hotel, the Australians provided General MacArthur with an automobile, a tall, long, shining black Wolseley limousine. Crowds gathered whenever it appeared on the streets of Melbourne, for (as an American observer remarked) General MacArthur was an easy motorist to spot. On the front were his four stars, on the rear the license plate USA-1. He was also an easy general to spot, especially after he received his winter uniform from an Australian tailor. From his left shoulder strap, bearing the four stars of a full general, to his breast pocket were ten rows of ribbons.

The limousine was usually bound for Victoria Barracks, the Australian Army headquarters, where War Council meetings were held. At the time discussions began with the Australians, MacArthur had been informed by cables from the United States that the men and matériel he needed would not be given him.

The decision had been made to defeat Germany first. Only two U.S. infantry divisions were promised him, both National Guard divisions not yet fully trained; the 41st was to arrive on April 6, the 32d the first week in May. The Australians could offer about 250,000 militia (the counterpart of the American National Guard) but they lacked training and equipment. The division of the A.I.F. (Australian Imperial Forces) sent home from the Middle East was assembling near Melbourne; but a brigade from another A.I.F. Division from the Middle East was on its way to Darwin.

With only these meager resources to depend upon, MacArthur was given by the U.S. Joint Chiefs of Staff on March 30 a vast area to retake – or defend. His Southwest Pacific Area extended as far north as the Philippines, as far west as the Netherlands East Indies, and as far east as the Solomon Islands, just southeast of the Bismarcks. On the northernmost of the Solomons, Buka and Bougainville, the Japanese had landed in mid-March.

All the rest of the Pacific Ocean came under a U.S. Navy commander, Admiral Chester W. Nimitz, headquarters Hawaii. His theater, Pacific Ocean Areas, was subdivided into North, Central, and – directly to the east of Australia – South Pacific, which comprised a string of small islands that were vital to the supply lines from the United States – New Caledonia, the Fijis, and Samoa – and also New Zealand, where the South Pacific's

2

commander, Vice Admiral Robert L. Ghormley, had his headquarters. No Japanese landings had yet taken place in the South Pacific.

At the time General MacArthur assumed command of the Southwest Pacific Area, Japanese bombers were roaring over the tail of the hovering New Guinea dragon, the tail that was Australia's territory of Papua. Their target was the territorial capital, Port Moresby, located on the underside of the tail facing Australia across the Coral Sea.

To MacArthur and the Australian staffs at Victoria Barracks in Melbourne, this seemed the point of greatest danger. If the Japanese captured Port Moresby, they could use it as a springboard for an invasion of Australia.

A small copra port with a vast blue-green harbor ringed by bare brown hills, Port Moresby at the end of March lay open to capture by land or sea. At a dusty airfield in the hills, an Australian squadron had only five or six planes operable of its original seventeen American Kittyhawk fighters, no match for Japanese Zeros. Port Moresby itself was a ghost town, its 2,000 Australian inhabitants having been evacuated, its native population having disappeared into the interior, its garrison of raw militiamen sent back into the hills to work on airfield construction. At the waterfront, blazing in the tropical heat, where flimsy wooden stores and warehouses lay splintered by Japanese bombs, the only protection was a battery of two antiquated coastal guns pointing toward the empty harbor.

On the land side, Port Moresby was protected by a great mountain barrier, the towering jungle-clad chain of the Owen Stanley Range, running the length of the tail. On the map, a line showed a passage over the mountains from Port Moresby to Buna, an Australian outpost on the Solomon Sea facing Rabaul; on that desolate palm-fringed upper coast were only two small Australian settlements: Buna Government Station (near a native village named Buna) and, 10 miles to the north, a long-established Anglican mission at Gona.

MacArthur called the passage over the mountains a 'route'; the Japanese (who were also studying the map) called it a 'road'. In fact, the route from Port Moresby as far as Kokoda, a hill station in the foothills on the Solomon Sea side, was only a footpath two or three feet wide, used by barefoot natives or an occasional missionary. It climbed mountains as high as 6,000 feet, clung to the side of gorges, descended to cross brawling streams on moss-covered stones or logs, then ascended to heights of misty rain forest. This ancient native footpath was to become famous as the Kokoda Track.

The few Australians who had ever been to New Guinea (it is five hours by air from Melbourne) scoffed at the idea that the Kokoda Track could be used for an invasion; but Australian military planners took it seriously, considering the Buna–Gona area a major threat because it was 'the northern terminus of the one "good" track to Port Moresby'.

Not by land, however, but by sea came the first invasion attempt.

On May 3 the Japanese occupied Tulagi in the lower Solomons and next day their troop transports steamed south down the Solomon Sea, protected by aircraft carriers. But the Allies had been warned by the Australian Navy's Coastwatching Service, manned by planters and civil servants who had taken to the hills and set up wireless stations within the enemy lines; and by U.S. Naval Intelligence whose cryptanalysts had cracked the Japanese naval code.

As the Japanese fleet heading for Port Moresby was entering the Coral Sea off the tip of the New Guinea tail, it was intercepted by aircraft and ships from both the Southwest and South Pacific Areas and a strange naval battle followed in which the opposing ships never saw each other – the damage was done by dive bombers launched from carriers. Both sides suffered badly in the Battle of the Coral Sea, but the result was that the Japanese forces withdrew and Port Moresby was saved.

But only for the moment. Nobody doubted that the enemy would try again; and while the Battle of the Coral Sea was taking place between May 5 and 8, the Philippines surrendered. This meant that the Japanese could release new forces for a further effort.

When the news of the fall of the Philippines came to the Bataan gang in Melbourne, 'we saw one another's tears,' one of them later recorded. General MacArthur, though he had predicted doom, was deeply affected by the surrender. For him personally it was a defeat, and he could not bear the thought of another defeat in this new theater. Pointing out to Australian Prime Minister John Curtin that there were present in the

Southwest Pacific 'all of the elements that have produced disaster in the Western Pacific since the beginning of the war,' he pleaded for speedy reinforcements: at least two aircraft carriers, an increase in U.S. air strength from 500 to 1,000 planes, and a U.S. army corps of three first-class divisions.

He might as well have asked for the moon. These forces were not available, especially the carriers, and especially at that moment. Cryptanalysts had discovered that the Japanese were planning to move against the Aleutians and Midway Island northwest of Hawaii, their purpose to knock out the U.S. fleet. All the resources of the U.S. Navy in the Pacific were being drawn upon to defeat this attack.

Lacking carriers, MacArthur decided to establish an airfield on the southeastern coast of New Guinea from which land-based bombers and fighters could attack an invasion convoy as it rounded the tip of the New Guinea tail. A reconnaissance party sent to the area in a Catalina flying boat recommended Milne Bay, a long narrow bight that forked the tip of the tail. At the head of the bay a coconut plantation developed by Lever Brothers before the war had a small landing field, a road net, and some jetties.

At the time the favorable report came in, Milne Bay assumed new importance. The Battle of Midway on June 7 had resulted in a smashing victory for the U.S. fleet and dealt the Japanese Navy a blow from which it could probably not recover. The Allies could now go on the offensive.

On June 8 MacArthur proposed a bold attack on Rabaul using bases on the coast of New Guinea and in the southern Solomons. The plan received considerable attention by the Joint Chiefs of Staff in Washington throughout June; and considerable modification at the hands of the U.S. Navy, which insisted on retaining control of amphibious operations. The result of the Joint Chiefs' deliberations was a directive on July 2 dividing the operation into three tasks. The Solomons had priority. Task One was 'seizure and occupation of the Santa Cruz Islands, Tulagi and adjacent positions'. Long after the Santa Cruz Islands and Tulago had been forgotten, an 'adjacent position' would be remembered. It was Guadalcanal, across from Tulagi, a large island with a flat space for an airfield.

Responsibility for Task One was given to Admiral Ghormley, with a target date of August 1; on that date Tulagi and adjacent positions were to be transferred from the Southwest Pacific to the South Pacific Area. Task Two, 'Seizure and occupation of the remainder of the Solomon Islands, of Lae, Salamaua, and the northeast coast of New Guinea,' and Task Three, 'Seizure and occupation of Rabaul and adjacent positions in the New Guinea–New Ireland area,' were given to MacArthur, without target date but with the warning that planning should be completed as soon as possible.

MacArthur lost no time in preparing for the attack on Lae and Salamaua and for this he needed an airfield north of Milne Bay. The logical place was Buna Government Station, which had a small landing strip.

As the Buna area was also the logical place for a Japanese landing, MacArthur had already taken precautions to secure it, especially to deny the enemy the 'route' through Kokoda to Port Moresby. For this purpose the Australian commander at Port Moresby had in June organized a force, called Maroubra Force, consisting of an Australian militia battalion, the 39th, and the Papuan Infantry Battalion.

The first element of Maroubra Force, Company B of the 39th Battalion, was by July 7 assembled at a plateau in the foothills some 30 miles north of Port Moresby, ready to start over the Owen Stanley Range. There the troops first saw the red ribbon of earth that was the Kokoda Track and had their first view of the blue-green mountains rising row on row.

These were the first troops ever to attempt the mountain crossing. They were to make it in conditions that would seem later, to their successors, almost luxurious. To carry their gear they had a force of 600 native Papuans, small brown men with frizzy hair (Papua in the native dialect means 'woolly'), naked except for loincloths or 'lap-laps'. And the troops had to guide them into the unknown mountain reaches a man who knew well the country and the people. He was Lieutenant Herbert T. Kienzle of the Australian New Guinea Administrative Unit (A.N.G.A.U.), who owned a rubber plantation near Kokoda. Kienzle set up staging camps along the way where the men could bivouac and rest.

Nevertheless, their climb over the Kokoda Track was agonizing. It took them eight days of hard climbing from the foothills at Port Moresby to the foothills at Kokoda – a distance of less than 100 air miles. When on July 15 the men of Company B descended from the cool mountain heights to the steaming green valley into which was thrust the plateau of Kokoda, they were hardly fit for combat. This was a circumstance that military planners in Australia might have done well to heed.

On the day the exhausted troops reached Kokoda, General MacArthur issued instructions for establishing his base at Buna, an operation he called Providence. It was tentatively scheduled for August 10, for by that time the U.S. Navy would presumably have seized Guadalcanal in the Solomons after its planned August 1 landing and would be ready to return to MacArthur the few Australian ships and American aircraft he had been able to contribute to the landing.

The movement of Buna Force to the coast was to begin on July 31, when four Australian infantry companies and a small party of U.S. engineers were to set forth on foot over the Kokoda Track. Arriving at Buna some ten days later, they were to secure the area and assist in the landing of the main body of the force, which was to come around by sea from Port Moresby in small coastal vessels under naval escort. Then worw was to begin on a large airfield.

This was not to be at Buna, because reconnaissance by seaplane had found the small strip there inadequate, but some 15 miles to the south at Dobodura, a grasy plain large enough to take bombers as well as fighters. The strictest secrecy was enjoined on all. To avoid detection by Japanese aircraft, not a blade of kunai grass was to be disturbed at Dobodura until Buna Force was safely ashore.

In his preparations for Providence, General MacArthur arranged to move his headquarters from Melbourne to Brisbane, the northernmost of the Australian capital cities. The journey was to be made by train.

At two o'clock on the afternoon of July 21, General MacArthur's special train stood waiting at Spencer Street Station. Walking up and down the platform, waiting for the general to arrive, were a dozen American and Australian war correspondents who were going along. Many had been present at this same platform exactly four months before when General MacArthur arrived from the Philippines. Now he was about to embark on the first step of his return. It was a historic moment.

For the newspapermen it was also a moment of bitter frustration, for the dramatic story would never pass the censors. The move to Brisbane was as secret as the move to Buna. This time there were no cheering crowds, no flash bulbs, only a double line of M.P.s and the train waiting on the tracks.

Opposite Platform No. 1 was the general's private coach. The finest the Australian government could offer, built for the Prince of Wales when he visited Australia, it was finished in maroon with the royal coat of arms emblazoned on each side; peering inside, the newspapermen could see fresh flowers on the tables. Ahead were four passenger coaches for the general's staff, the press, and the enlisted men; and three baggage cars. Between the baggage cars and the highly polished engine were two flat cars. On the first was tied down General MacArthur's Wolseley limousine, USA-1, the second bore General Sutherland's Cadillac.

A little after two o'clock the M.P.s came to a salute. General MacArthur walked through the iron gate to Platform No. 1, accompanied by Mrs MacArthur, his little son Arthur, and the child's Chinese nurse carrying several toys. As the general stepped aboard the train with his party, the American officer in charge of the train gave the signal and the wheels began moving.

The newspapermen in Car No. 3 waited to be invited into the private car for an informal talk – customary on special trains in the United States, even the President's train – but they never were. Nor did the general leave his car, either during two short operating stops or at the long stop at Albury, the junction where the gauge changed and the passengers had to transfer from the Victorian Railways to the New South Wales Railways.

On their seven o'clock arrival at Albury the passengers saw across the station platform the train that was to carry them to Sydney and on to Brisbane, its baggage cars and flat cars directly opposite those on the train from Melbourne, to facilitate loading. The detachment of Australian soldiers who had ben given the job of loading looked thoroughly fed up with the work involved. An hour later, when the correspondents returned to the train after an excellent dinner in the station dining-room, the soldiers looked even more unhappy. They had just moved USA-1 and still had to tackle the chairs, desks, and file cabinets in the baggage cars.

Behind the baggage cars of the Brisbane train was a string of

23

sleeping cars, ending with a special car for General MacArthur lent by the premier of New South Wales. Though highly varnished, it was nothing like as impressive as the car that had brought the general from Melbourne. But it had one feature that made the correspondents stare – its guards. At each corner of the car stood an American M.P., resplendent in white belt, white holster cord and white gloves, covering with a Tommy gun everyone who came near, even the Australian police. This performance, which was to be repeated at every stop, earned for the train the name by which it was thereafter referred to by the newspapermen: 'The Circus Train'.

Five minutes before departure time General MacArthur emerged from his Melbourne car, crossed the platform, waving to the news correpsondents, and entered his sleeping car. The train pulled out for Brisbane, 1,018 miles away. When it got under way the conductor came around handing out hot water bottles for the berths. The cars were unheated, in deference to the Australian belief that it never got cold enough for heaters; and the night was cold.

Frost was on the ground when they rolled into Sydney next morning. As the train entered the station and stopped, a Signal Corps detachment strung wire from the stationmaster's office to General MacArthur's car. Over the wire came momentous news. The Japanese were landing near Buna.

CHAPTER II

THE JAPANESE INVASION

At Gona Mission House on the afternoon of July 21, Sister May Hayman, the head nurse and housekeeper, put dinner in the oven and sat down with Sister Mavis Parkinson, the head teacher, to do some mending. The dining-room table was piled high with khaki shirts and shorts left behind by two young Australian soldiers who had stopped at Gona the night before, on their way from Buna Government Station to the wireless station at Ambasi 30 miles up the coast.

The soldiers liked to stop at Gona. It was the loveliest spot on the coast, a garden between beach and jungle. Overlooking a sweep of black beach sand and the blue waters of the Solomon Sea was a handsome church of gray woven sago-leaf; behind it the well-kept Mission House with a red tin roof that acted as a catchment for rainwater. A pretty schoolhouse with reedy walls of sago-stalk stood near a green cricket field. Yellow crotons and red hibiscus bordered the paths; palms and tall tulip trees shaded the grounds.

The beauty of Gona was not the only attraction. The two young Australian sisters and Father James Benson, the white-haired English priest, tried to provide an atmosphere of home for the soldiers. On the evening before, the girls put on long evening dresses and saw to it that dinner was served from a polished table with a centrepiece of flowers. After dinner they took their guests down to the front lawn, where the house boys had hung a lamp from a palm frond and set out deck chairs. They played the mission gramophone, watched the phosphorescence on the sea below, and passed around a box of chocolates that Mavis had just received from home.

One of the soldiers, gazing on the lamp hanging from the palm tree, said, 'I don't suppose many places in the world today dare show so much light as this.'

The war had not entirely bypassed Gona. Early in the year a dozen native canoes had brought a party of Australian refugees from Japanese-occupied Salamaua up the coast, and a Japanese seaplane had machine-gunned the beach to the south, near Buna. In June the body of an American pilot had fallen near the church, just before his plane crashed into the jungle beyond. But no bombs had fallen on Gona.

On the afternoon of July 21 while the girls were sewing in the dining-room of the Mission House, Father Benson was working in the carpenter's shop. A handsome, strongly built man of fifty-seven, with warm dark eyes behind steel-rimmed spectacles, he was repairing a small deck chair that he used on canoe journeys to his outlying stations, placing it on the woven bark platform of a native outrigger.

He had a huge parish, and in many ways a horrifying one. It included some of the most feared natives in New Guinea, the Orokaivas, the 'Spear Men' who had learned to make spears from the black palm. They were only fifty years removed from cannibalism, and that in a peculiarly revolting form – the practice of 'living meat', in which they tied their prisoners to a tree and as meat was needed cut slices from buttocks or legs, plastering pandanus leaves over the wounds; some of the poor wretches, Father Benson had learned, would live in agony for two weeks.

At the end of the nineteenth century white men seeking gold had come into the area and behaved brutally to the native women. The Spear Men rose up and massacred them and also killed the government forces sent to rescue them. Years later, after the founding of Gona Mission in 1900 on the spot where the massacre had taken place, some of the Orokaivas became Christians. But many retained a burning hatred of the whites.

Father Benson had just finished repairing his chair and was putting his tools away when he heard shouting down on the beach. Then a terror-stricken native boy appeared at the door of the workshop crying, 'Father! Father! Come quickly, there are big, big ships!'

Out in the sea, where nothing larger than the small mission ketch had ever appeared, stood a huge transport with a destroyer on either side and two cruisers farther out.

Father Benson made his way to the beach through a crowd of natives who were heading for the jungle, carrying their babies, sleeping mats, clay pots, and pigs. He was joined almost immediately by the two sisters, who came running from Mission House. They thought at first that the ships were Australian. Then the cruisers opened fire on the shore to the south and two or three planes with Australian markings came over and began bombing the transport, the deep boom of the explosions shaking the palm trees on the shore.

Sister Hayman said, 'Surely they won't come ashore here, they will go to Buna.'

As the three missionaries watched spellbound, as if watching a play, they saw boats lowered over the side of the transport and men tumbling into them. The destroyers began to shell Gona beach.

Shells were screaming over the mission buildings when the priest and the two girls, hastily gathering together some food, a compass, mosquito nets, and clothing, stole away down a track through the swamps behind Gona, heading toward an Anglican mission near Sangara Rubber Plantation in the foothills of the Owen Stanley Range. In the gathering darkness they crossed the narrow bridges spanning the swamp drains, then stumbled along for two hours in pitch-black darkness. Coming to a small clearing in the tall grass a little way off the track, they sat down to wait until the moon came up.

Two hours later they heard voices along the track and saw lights. A Japanese patrol with flashlights passed within a few feet of them and disappeared in the direction of Sangara. The missionaries' escape route was cut off. They decided to leave the track, with only their compass to guide them. Father Benson said the Itinerarium and the collect beginning, 'Lighten our darkness, O Lord,' and they plunged into the trackless jungle.

The soldiers with the flashlights were part of an advance patrol sent forward by Colonel Yosuke Yokoyama, the commander of the Japanese invasion forces. From the transport that Father Benson saw and two others that he did not see, Colonel Yokoyama landed almost 2,000 troops. Most of them were engineers, but he also had a battalion of infantry, a company of marines from the 5th Sasebo Landing Forces, detachments from mountain artillery and antiaircraft units, and a number of supporting troops.

His mission was to prepare the way for the main Japanese force, Major General Tomitaro Horii's South Seas Detachment (in Japanese, Nankai Shitai), conquerors of Rabaul and, before that, Guam. Horii's élite corps of jungle fighters was to be reinforced later by another crack outfit, the Yazawa Force, veterans of Malaya, where they had shared in the victory at Singapore.

Colonel Yokoyama's orders were to put the road from Buna to Kokoda in condition to handle motor traffic and to prepare the 'road' across the Owen Stanley Range for trucks if possible, but in any case for pack horses. And so ignorant were the Japanese of what lay before them in the mountains – indeed they knew little of New Guinea, regarding it as a 'dark, uncivilized place' – that when Horii arrived a month later he brought 400 pack horses to use on the Kokoda Track. Yokoyama landed more than 50, as well as 1,200 Rabaul natives to act as carriers.

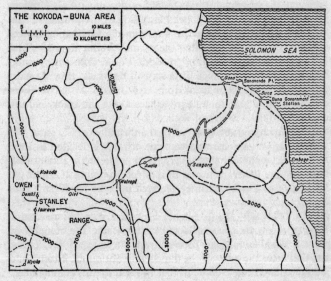

THE KOKODA – BUNA AREA

The invasion force quickly spread out. The troops of one party made for Gona, where they found at Mission House Sister Hayman's dinner still hot in the oven. At the schoolhouse they gathered up the children's exercise books and turned them over to officers of the Kempai (military police), who began frantically searching them for military information.

The main Japanese base was not to be at Gona, but at a point down the coast, almost halfway between Gona and Buna, called Sanananda, which had been the shipping point for Sangara Rubber plantation, some 25 miles back from the coast in the foothills. From their warehouse as Sanananda the plantation managers had built a corduroy road that ran for about 15 miles inland. This the Japanese knew. In the first landings, army troops were put ashore at Sanananda to build the base. The following morning, marines were landed at Buna to build airfields.

In the landing at Buna, two transports were damaged by Allied planes, but a heavy haze protected the other vessels and by noon on July 22 all invasion ships were on their way back to Rabaul to pick up reinforcements.

At Buna Government Station on the afternoon of July 21, two young Australian officers and several native soldiers of the Papuan Constabulary saw a Japanese cruiser shelling the beach at Sanananda and tried to report by radio to Port Moresby but the radio was dead. Leaving Buna a little before six o'clock, barely escaping an attack by Japanese bombers, they stopped at Sangara to warn the plantation people and missionaries, then traveled all night toward the nearest constabulary headquarters, which was at a village called Awala at a place where the track inland began to ascend to Kokoda.

Another traveler hurrying along the track to Awala that night was the commander of B Company, which had marched over the mountains, Captain Samuel V. Templeton. A man in his fifties who had served in submarines in World War I and had fought in Spain during the Spanish Civil War, he was greatly beloved by his troops, who called him 'Uncle Sam'. Finding the garrison at Awala already alerted, he ordered forward to Awala one of his platoons at Kokoda. Next day, learning that after the news of the Japanese invasion the entire 39th Battalion had been ordered to Kokoda and that its commander,

Colonel W. T. Owen, was on his way by air, Templeton left for Kokoda to meet Owen, leaving the Australian commander of the native battalion, Major W. T. Watson, in charge at Awala.

About four o'clock on the afternoon of July 23, just as the reinforcements from Kokoda were arriving, the Japanese were seen coming down the road to Awala. They wore green uniforms and steel helmets garnished with leaves. Some were on bicycles. Each carried in addition to his arms and ammunition a machete for cutting through the jungle, a mess tin of cooked rice, and a shovel slung over his back. They were professionals. When a small patrol engaged them as they approached Awala, they threw out flanking patrols and brought down heavy fire from machine guns, mortars, and a field gun.

The native soldiers melted away into the jungle – 'went bush' – and the Australians fell back across the swift Kumusi River at the place where a narrow footbridge was suspended from a wire rope (the natives called the place Wairopi). They destroyed the bridge behind them, but this did not stop the swift and deadly Japanese pursuit. Next morning the Japanese bridged the river and pressed forward, climbing trees along the track from which they poured down sniper fire on the Australians attempting to stop them.

By the afternoon of July 25, Templeton's two platoons had fallen back to Oivi, a village only a two-hour march from Kokoda. At five o'clock Captain Templeton left for Kokoda to bring up reinforcements. Ten minutes after he left there was the sharp crack of a rifle from the jungle. He was never seen again.

By nightfall the enemy had encircled Oivi. The men of B Company, already exhausted from their climb over the Owen Stanleys, were on the edge of collapse; most had had little rest or food for four days; some were falling asleep over their weapons. Around ten o'clock Major Watson decided to withdraw. Guided by a native police boy, in the blackness of night with heavy rain falling, the party slipped through the Japanese lines and found a track that bypassed Kokoda and led to Deniki, a native village just to the south of it on the Kokoda Track. There they were joined on July 27 by Lieutenant Colonel Owen, with his small force, who had found Kokoda untenable after the encirclement at Oivi.

During the day there walked into Deniki a notable figure on

the Kokoda Track, Dr Geoffrey Hamden Vernon. One of the best known of the 'old hands' in New Guinea, both as doctor and planter, he was sixty years old and quite deaf, but had refused to leave the area when the older people were evacuated. A tireless walker, he had lately been acting as medical officer to the native carrier line and had just walked over the Kokoda Track on his first tour of inspection. He found Deniki cheerless and cold that night. In the improvised aid post, he did not have the comfort of a single blanket; the wind blew chill through the gaps in the floor of the native hut and a shower of water fell through the thatched roof.

Next morning, good news came. A patrol reported that the Japanese had not yet occupied Kokoda. Owen hastened back to Kokoda, accompanied by Dr Vernon, with a force consisting of most of his Australians and the remnant of his native constabulary, in all about eighty men. He disposed his forces around the tongue of the plateau, where the track from Oivi climbed up and where he naturally expected the attack. At noon two planes came over. They carried Owen's reinforcements; but the pilots, after receiving a message that Kokoda had been abandoned, circled the field and returned to Port Moresby.

At dusk no Japanese had yet appeared. Dr Vernon went into the deserted house of an old friend, where he had often been entertained, lay down on a sofa, and was joined by the family's yellow cat. He fed it a piece of scone, it nestled against him, and they both fell asleep. Because of his deafness he was unaware of the Japanese attack that came early in the evening. He slept on until midnight when he was awakened by a touch on his shoulder. Lieutenant Colonel Owen had been shot in the act of throwing a grenade from a firing pit at the edge of the escarpment.

Though a white mountain mist had come up, the moon was full, and by its light they found Owen. Vernon saw that the skull and brain had been penetrated and that there was no hope for him. Orders then came for all to retreat at once. Against the eighty men, the Japanese had brought to bear a force of about four hundred. Their mortars bombarded the plateau and sometime during the night they brought up their 70-mm. support gun.

The mist protected the withdrawal. Vernon never forgot 'The

thick white mist dimming the moonlight; the mysterious veiling of trees, houses, and men, the drip of moisture from the foliage, and at the last the almost complete silence, as if the rubber groves of Kokoda were sleeping as usual in the depths of the night, and men had not brought disturbance.'

Returning to the rain-drenched huts and water-filled weapon pits of Deniki, the battered remnant of B Company settled in to await reinforcements. On August 1 two companies of the 39th Battalion walked in. Moreover, hope of replacing the food and ammunition lost at Kokoda was brought by Lieutenant Kienzle. His climb over the Kokoda Track with B Company had convinced him that the troops could not be supplied by native carriers alone; supplies would have to be dropped by airplanes; and he had solved the problem of finding a dropping ground in the mountains.

Remembering that on flights from Kokoda to Port Moresby before the war he had noticed a wide green valley as his plane passed over the crest of the Owen Stanleys, he had set out on foot to find it, accompanied by four natives. When they reached the summit of the main range, he saw his green valley lying to the southeast. The natives hesitated. They told him the valley was taboo, a place of ghosts. But Kienzle persuaded them to continue. They camped at dusk beside a creek and built a fire, for at that altitude the jungle air was chill after dark. Early next morning they emerged from the jungle onto the forbidden ground, a flat expanse of open country about a mile long and half a mile wide, covered with waving green kunai grass. Set like a saucer in the mountain range, it was the dry bed of an old lake; a sparkling stream cut across its center. Quail started up and the harsh cry of wild duck broke the stillness.

The place had no name. Kienzle called it Myola, the name of the wife of an old friend. It is an Australian aboriginal word meaning 'dawn of day'. He reported his discovery of Myola over the telephone line which had just been laid from Port Moresby over the mountains, and asked that air dropping begin immediately.

The completion of the telephone line on August 4 made the men at Deniki feel less isolated. More important, on that day Maroubra Force received a vigorous new commander, Major Alan Cameron, one of the A.I.F. officers who had escaped from Rabaul. Two days later all companies of the 39th Battalion were on hand, a total of 464 men. With the small force of native soldiers, Cameron had 533 men. He decided at once on a bold atempt to recapture Kokoda, intending by a swift surprise attack to throw the Japanese off balance, gain the airfield, and be reinforced by air.

On the morning of August 8, three companies moved out in the attack. Two were repulsed and had to withdraw to Deniki, but the third, infiltrating by a little-known track that entered the plateau through the rubber plantation, reached Kokoda shortly after noon without encountering any opposition. Emerging from the rubber plantation, the men saw only four or five Japanese standing by the administration buildings. With a cry of alarm, these fled.

The Australians dug in around the plateau, reconnoitered the airfield, and at dusk fired a Very flare from the center of the runway – the prearranged signal that the mission had been accomplished. That night the Japanese did not attack.

Heavy rain began during the night and was still falling next morning. At ten o'clock the Japanese came creeping through the rubber plantation, smeared with mud and hard to distinguish through the shadows and the rain. They were stopped by heavy fire; and when they resumed the attack after dark, crawling on hands and knees, they were again repulsed. At daylight an airplane circled Kokoda. The Australians waved their slouch hats to identify themselves, but the plane gave no sign of recognition and flew away.

The Japanese, believing that airplanes would soon be landing reinforcements, reacted strongly. At dusk from their positions on the edge of the plateau came a weird, dirge-like chanting. As the cadences, rising and falling, died away in the dusk, a Japanese officer called out in perfect English, 'You don't fancy that, do you?'

The Australians yelled, 'Never heard worse!' But they soon found out that the chant had to be taken seriously. On that day and on later occasions when it was heard along the Kokoda Track, it presaged a strong attack. Fire rained down from mortars and heavy machine guns, and the enemy stormed the plateau.

The Australians, lacking reinforcements by air, had to withdraw; food and ammunition were running out. After dark they slipped into the jungle at the edge of the airfield. There they spent the night, sodden, cold, and hungry. Next morning they took a track that led in a roundabout way back to Deniki and on the second day reached a native garden, made a fire, its smoke lost in the swirling mist, and cooked a stew of bananas, pumpkins, and sugar cane. Plodding on the following day, August 12, they came at noon to a native village where the chieftain provided a dinner of roasted sweet potatoes. Ravenously snatching the sweet potatoes half-roasted from the coals, they lay down on the rain-drenched ground and slept.

When they neared Deniki on August 13, they learned that the village was under heavy attack. They went on to the next village up the Kokoda Track, Isurava. There they were joined next day by the rest of Cameron's forces, which had been routed from Deniki under such pressure that they had to abandon their food, blankets, and most of their equipment. Digging in at Isurava, using as tools their bayonets, steel helmets, and bully-beef tins, they formed a perimeter and determined to make a stand.

While the Japanese were advancing into the mountains, their big ships continued to land men and supplies on the beaches between Gona and Buna. One convoy was recalled to Rabaul when news came of the American landing on Guadalcanal on August 7; but after the Japanese victory at sea in the Solomons on August 9, when the Allied fleet had been forced to withdraw after losing four cruisers, the convoy was again dispatched and arrived safely off Buna on August 13.

Five days later there arrived three escorted troop transports carrying the main body of General Horii's South Sea Detachment, followed on August 21 by the first elements of Yazawa Force. In the month since the first big ships had come in on July 21, the Japanese landed in the Gona-Buna area 8,000 army troops, 3,000 naval construction troops, and some 450 marines.

The coastal plain between Buna and Kokoda was securely in Japanese hands. Australians hiding in the jungle had been betrayed by natives and harshly dealt with. Natives seized the party from Sangara – the plantation manager, two priests, two sisters, a lay mission worker, a half-caste plantation assistant with his six-year-old son, and a young half-caste woman – mistreated them and then handed them over to the Japanese. All were beheaded with a sword by a Japanese marine officer

34

on the beach at Buna, the small boy last of all.

Father Benson, Mavis Parkinson, and May Hayman, after being forced off the track and into the jungle on the night of July 21 had turned north and found refuge at a mission outstation on the lower Kumusi River. They stayed there until August 9, when rumors that the Japanese were advancing led them to join a party of men who were attempting to reach Port Moresby by making a wide swing over the mountains east of Kokoda; they were five Australian soldiers who had been manning the wireless station at Ambasi, and five Americans who were pilots and crews of two fighter planes shot down over the jungle.

One of the Americans had a leg wound and was on crutches. The two sisters' shoes were thin and badly worn. Starting out on August 10, all traveled painfully and slowly and were very tired when they reached the point of greatest danger, a Japanese camp on the Sanananda Road. There they were betrayed by a native guide and on August 15 were attacked by the Japanese. Father Benson, who had become separated from the party in the gloom of the jungle, heard rifle fire, then a burst from the Tommy gun the Americans were carrying. The firing died down and the priest was sure all had escaped.

As he hoped, they did get away that night, but two days later they were surrounded by hostile natives and handed over to the Japanese. All were killed except the two girls and an Australian lieutenant, who managed to escape into the jungle. But somehow the girls became separated from the Australian officer and again were betrayed by natives. The Japanese took them to an open field where a trench had been dug. There Mavis Parkinson and May Hayman were bayoneted to death.

Father Benson wandered in the jungle for four days before he came out on the road to Sanananda. He had resolved to surrender, and to prove he was not a soldier he took his white cassock out of his shoulder pouch and put it on over his shirt and khaki shorts. Coming out of the jungle into the sunlight, he saw Japanese soldiers sitting in a clearing eating rice. He walked over to an officer and said, 'I am the priest of Gona.' The officer said, 'Spy!' and waved him away.

The day was August 20. Horii's troops had just landed. Soldiers were marching down the road, four deep; then came guns, and finally ammunition carried by Rabaul natives. At one point a hundred small boys marched by, each with a single shell on his shoulder. Then more infantrymen. As they passed along they paid no attention to Father Benson's plea, 'Does anybody speak English?'

At last an officer replied, 'Oh yes, quite a lot of us can speak English if we want to.'

'Then please help me. I am the priest of Gona.'

'I have no time for whites.'

'But you are allied to the Germans.'

'I have no time for the Germans either,' said the officer, and walked on.

Unable to find anyone who would take the trouble to permit him to surrender, Father Benson walked up the road toward the sea until he came to a rest house where he encountered a friendly quartermaster who gave him rice and some herring in tomato sauce from a can he recognized as coming from the Mission House at Gona.

Next morning he hopped on a truck that was headed toward Sanananda. It was filled with soldiers. When they found out he was British, they began singing, 'It's a Long Way to Tipperary'; he later discovered that they had a craze for learning English songs.

At Sanananda, where he found huge dumps being established, he managed to surrender to Colonel Yokoyama himself, a short fat man in a yellow kimono, resembling so much the famous statue of the sitting Buddha that Father Benson always thought of him as 'the fat placid Buddha of the Kimono'. His next encounter with Yokoyama was less formal. One day when he went to bathe in a river where the Japanese had railed off a pool in the shadows, he found the colonel sitting alone in the swirling waters. Looking up smiling, he beckoned the priest into the water and handed him a cake of perfumed soap. As they bathed, Father Benson discovered that the colonel had the few words of English possessed by most of the Japanese, and enjoyed practicing them. He encouraged the priest to talk of England and responded, 'Ah! England like Nippon, varie boot-ee-ful, okay! okay!'

Father Benson spent several months at the Japanese base camp before he was taken by ship to Rabaul, and on the whole he was not badly treated. In the days following his arrival at Sanananda on August 21 he discovered that the

Japanese were puzzled by the lack of opposition, by land or air, to their landings. They were full of confidence. Almost as soon as he arrived they told him they were nearing Port Moresby, and before long he was informed that the port had been captured.

Every night the radio operator in his tent could be heard calling: 'Hello! Hello! Port Moresby! Port Moresby!' This Father Benson realized later was propaganda directed at their own troops in the base camp. But it was credible: 'They had captured places like Manila and Singapore with little apparent difficulty; why not Port Moresby?'

CHAPTER III

MILNE BAY:
NIGHT BATTLES IN THE RAIN

An American officer reporting to General MacArthur at his headquarters in Brisbane on August 1, 1942, observed that the general looked 'tired, drawn, and nervous.'

The officer was Major General George C. Kenney, a small, cocky Air Force general who had been sent from the United States to take over from Lieutenant General George H. Brett the command of Allied Air Forces. Brett's failure to stop the Japanese landings on the Buna coast seemed to MacArthur ample justification for the decision he had already made to relieve him. Kenney was greeted by a tirade against the Air Forces.

Defeat, Brett commented later, 'raked his spirit raw.'

Moreover, an ominous cable had just come from Washington. General George C. Marshall, U.S. Army Chief of Staff, demanded to know what MacArthur was doing to stop the Japanese invasion.

In the next few days he was able to reply that he had ordered to New Guinea the crack Australian 7th Division, veterans of the Middle East, two brigades to Port Moresby, the third to Milne Bay. These regulars, along with the Australian militia and the small U.S. contingent of air crews, engineers, and antiaircraft men, were designated New Guinea Force and put under the command of Lieutenant General Sydney F. Rowell, a tall, lean, hawk-nosed professional soldier who had served with distinction in the Middle East. Rowell's mission was to hold the Owen Stanley Range, then retake Buna.

Ambitious plans! Neither General MacArthur nor General Sir Thomas Blamey, the Australian who commanded Allied Land Forces, had even seen the Owen Stanley Range or had much comprehension of the hardships of the Kokoda Track. Moreover, when the 7th Division men began landing at Port Moresby a formidable supply crisis had arisen. There were not enough native porters to carry food and ammunition over the mountains. Planes could drop supplies at Myola, the beautiful upland valley at the crest; but on the five-day climb to Myola the troops would have to carry their own rations and ammunition.

By August 15 the advance battalions were assembled at a rubber plantation in the foothills of the Owen Stanleys, ready to march. Visiting them there, General Rowell found them in high spirits, sharpening their bayonets on a plantation grindstone. He told them, 'I don't think I have ever given any troops a tougher job than this.'

When they took to the Kokoda Track on August 16, some of them were carrying loads up to 70 pounds. The strain soon began to tell. The following day their commander, Brigadier Arnold W. Potts, a thickset, round-faced man of forty-six with crewcut gray hair, passed men lying panting on the ground, utterly exhausted. Those who forced themselves to keep going were supporting their shaking legs with limbs cut from trees.

Potts, unencumbered, made good time and reached Myola on August 21. There he made an appalling discovery. The 40,000 rations promised him had not arrived. A Japanese air raid on Port Moresby had destroyed, on the ground, all but one of the supply-laden transports. General MacArthur was planning to use bombers for the airdrop; but until they could deliver enough supplies to furnish a 30-day reserve, the offensive could not be launched.

In a drenching rain that turned the track into soupy mud, Potts left Myola and went forward to visit the young militiamen of the 39th Battalion, positioned astride the track at cold, mist-shrouded Isurava.

He was shocked by their condition. Weary from fighting, and from long vigils in their cheerless weapon pits, soaked by the hard rains that fell every afternoon, depleted by casualties and malaria and weak from hunger, they had, according to their commander, 'literally come to a standstill.'

Potts decided to send the militiamen back to Port Moresby as soon as a battalion of regulars could arrive from Myola. But it was soon apparent that he would need every man he had. On the day after he arrived at Isurava, a forward patrol was attacked by a party of Japanese. By August 26 it was certain that the Japanese were launching an offensive. As soon as the morning mists had lifted, they brought up mountain artillery, shelled Isurava, and hurled an attack up the track. The militiamen beat them off. During the afternoon the first elements of the regulars arrived; the position at Isurava held. But shortly after dark, artillery shells began to fall on Potts's headquarters a mile to the rear. He sent off by wireless a plea for reinforcements from Port Moresby.

Early next morning came the answer. No reinforcements could be sent. Port Moresby itself was threatened. On the morning of August 26 the Japanese had landed at Milne Bay.

In the gloomy dusk of August 24, after heavy tropical rain had been drumming on the tin roofs of Milne Bay for four days, a drenched and breathless radio operator came running to the headquarters shack with an alarming message. A 'coast-watcher' south of Buna reported seeing seven 50-foot landing barges loaded with Japanese soldiers moving down the coast toward Milne Bay.

At first light next morning the commander of Milne Force, Major General Cyril A. Clowes, sent his Kittyhawk fighter-bombers to look for the barges. The Kittyhawks spotted them drawn up on the beach at Goodenough Island and, swooping low, destroyed them; but worse news came later in the morning. Aircraft over the Buna area reported a large Japanese naval force, including three cruisers and two transports, heading toward Milne Bay. Then the convoy disappeared under a heavy cloud cover that protected it from attack by heavy bombers. Later in the afternoon, when it came within fighter range, the Kittyhawks dived under the clouds to attack, but were driven off by intensive antiaircraft fire. Then darkness closed in.

There was not much General Clowes could do. A man cautious and taciturn, he had served with distinction in Greece – but this dismal battleground was nothing like Greece. On most of the great arc that formed the head of Milne Bay,

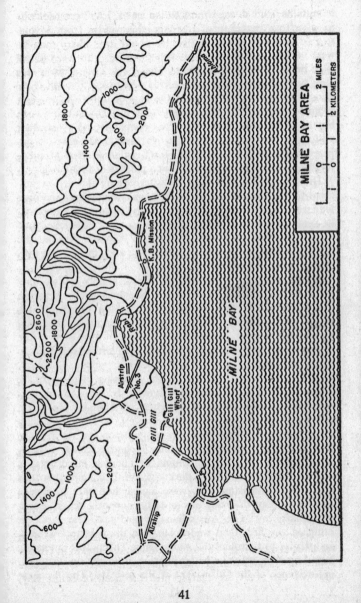

MILNE BAY AREA

2 MILES

2 KILOMETERS

MILNE BAY

K. B. Mission

Airstrip No. 3

Gili Gili Wharf

Gili Gili

Airstrip

mountains came down almost to the water, leaving room only for a narrow coastal road. The exception was the coastal plain around Gili Gili, about the center of the arc; slightly to the west of Gili Gili was the airstrip on which the Kittyhawks were based. This seemed the best area for defense. Clowes had already sited there his newly arrived veterans of the 7th Division, placing his militiamen to the east of Gili Gili, on high ground where another airstrip (Airstrip No. 3) was being built by the American engineers. Two companies of Australian militiamen were strung out even farther to the east on the narrow coastal shelf, one at K. B. (Kristian Bruder) Mission, the other – most exposed of all – at a place called Ahioma.

The Japanese might land anywhere along the arc at any time. Clowes had no navy, only a Royal Australian Air Force tender and a few mission luggers. On the evening of August 25 he sent the tender out to patrol the bay and dispatched two luggers to bring back the company at Ahioma. Around the Gili Gili wharf he set up a beach defense area, manning it with his American engineers.

About midnight the sound of heavy gunfire rolled over Milne Bay. It came from Ahioma, where the Japanese invasion was taking place. One of the luggers, taking off part of the Australian company, ran into Japanese landing parties and was heavily shelled. The second managed to turn back to the shore, where its passengers joined the men left behind in making for the jungle.

Shortly after one o'clock on the morning of August 26, the sentry of a patrol sent east from K. B. Mission saw four men approaching from the direction of Ahioma. Uncertain who they were, in the darkness and the rain, the sentry challenged them and they shot him. Thereupon the Australians shot the men approaching – four Japanese scouts. Twenty minutes later they saw a column of about a hundred men coming toward them in the darkness. On the chance that they might be Australians, they were hailed, but were then seen gathering about the body of one of the Japanese scouts, excitedly chattering. The Australians opened fire. The Japanese returned the fire, then waded out into the bay neck-deep in an attempt to surround the Australians. This failed; but as the patrol made its way to a better position, its leader saw astonishing evidence of the full weight of the invasion. The Japanese had tanks. A tank came down the road, first firing into the jungle on either side and then falling back so that the infantry could advance. The Australians hastened back to K. B. Mission to spread the word.

Antitank guns were sent for, but could not get through the mud. Reinforcements could bring only some antitank mines and 'sticky grenades'. With these, the Australian militiamen waited for the onslaught expected at daylight. It did not come, to their astonishment. They had not yet learned the invaders' pattern, to rest by day and fight by night.

That evening, about ten o'clock, the clouds thinned, and in the eerie dim moonlight the enemy launched a strong attack. Bullets rattled the stiff palm fronds. Suddenly a sheet of blinding flame from a flame-thrower illuminated the jungle and flashed on the water. The Japanese pressed on, wading into the sea on one side and into the swamp on the other to outflank the Australians. As they moved around the flanks they called out orders, in English, to stop firing and withdraw: 'It is no use resisting any longer.'

In later battles at Milne Bay the Australians were merely amused by such shouts, especially when the Japanese called out in the middle of the night, 'Who goes there? Friend. Good morning!' But in this first battle, some fifty men were deceived and moved back along the beach trail to Gili Gili. Shortly before dawn a genuine order came to withdraw a mile to the west, behind a river which would stop the tanks.

Next day things seemed better. The Japanese had vanished. In the afternoon the weary militiamen – many had had no sleep since the fighting began, and most were feverish with malaria – were relieved by the forward battalion of 7th Division regulars. On the way to the front, the commander of these Middle East veterans had heard an alarming rumor that 5,000 Japanese had been landed the first day. On arrival at K. B. Mission he placed his men in loose perimeter defense and hoped for the best. They were there, waiting for the attack, at nightfall on August 27.

Shortly before midnight out of the darkness a tank appeared, its headlights shining through the rain. Then the Australians heard the same kind of chanting that had been heard at Kokoda. As Japanese infantrymen pressed forward, a second tank came down the road. Both tanks cruised around the

43

perimeter, flooding each other with their lights as protection against attack, raking the jungle with fire, and paving the way for infantrymen. Against them the Australians' sticky grenades, which had become moldy, were ineffective.

By midnight the Japanese were inside K. B. Mission. The defenders put up a hard fight and took heavy losses but were forced back, most into the jungle, the rest to the far bank of the river, where they set up a defensive position. No weapons could be brought forward by land, because pouring rain made the road from the rear a morass, but during the night a launch came in from the bay with an antitank rifle. With this a corporal got off a few shots when a tank, on which infantrymen were riding, surged up the track around two o'clock next morning; but the corporal was wounded and the position at the river was overrun. The officer in charge, believing that he was facing a force of 5,000 Japanese, ordered a withdrawal to the west.

Before dawn on August 28 the Japanese had crossed the river, where they had to leave their tanks, bogged down in the mud, and were approaching Airstrip No. 3, defended by an Australian militia battalion. Fortunately for the Australians, two cleared areas at the airstrip provided them with excellent fields of fire. They held firm. At daylight the Japanese withdrew, to hide in the jungle during the day.

That morning, August 28, General Clowes learned of the repercussions in Australia of the Japanese landings at Milne Bay. On August 26, in a conference with General Blamey, General MacArthur said he believed the Japanese would reinforce their landing by August 29. He advised offensive action before this could happen. Blamey that day urged Rowell to spur Clowes; but because of defective communications the orders from Australia to Port Moresby to Milne Bay took two days. Specific orders came late on August 28. As a result of peremptory instructions from MacArthur to 'clear the north shore of Milne Bay without delay,' Rowell ordered Clowes to 'put everything in.'

This Clowes was preparing to do, ordering the remaining two battalions of his 7th Division regulars to advance from the Gili Gili area eastward to K. B. Mission, when, late on the afternoon of August 29, he received a report from a reconnaissance aircraft that a Japanese cruiser and nine destroyers were heading for Milne Bay. On the chance that they might be intending to land in the Gili Gili area, the cautious Clowes canceled the orders to his regulars.

General MacArthur's intelligence had been correct. The cruiser and destroyers were escorting a convoy that brought the first major Japanese reinforcements since the invasion. On the night of August 29, protected by a heavy mist, the ships landed at the Japanese base between K. B. Mission and Ahioma nearly eight hundred men of the crack Japanese Special Naval Landing Forces.

General Clowes again ordered his regulars eastward; but as they were just setting out on the five-mile trek in the early hours of August 31, the Japanese launched a furious assault, shouting, against the seaward end of Airstrip No. 3.

The Australian militiamen were ready for them, having prepared a strong artillery and mortar defense, backed by American 50-mm. machine guns and two 37-mm. pieces manned by American engineers. With a good field of fire across the strip, the defenders threw back three attacks. Then the Japanese moved around to the northern end of the strip, but came up against another excellent defensive position sited on high ground, and were finally repulsed. Just before dawn a Japanese bugle sounded three times in the darkness – the signal to call off the attack.

The first elements of the regulars sent forward, slowed by the deep mud, so deep that the men sank to their knees in it, did not reach the strip until midmorning. Crossing the strip, they came under Japanese fire from snipers in trees, from parties hidden in the jungle along the road, and even from Japanese who lay motionless among their own dead until the Australians passed by, then rose and fired on them from the rear.

Delayed but not stopped by these tactics, the first battalion of 7th Division regulars was by midafternoon storming K. B. Mission at bayonet point, killing about sixty Japanese. That night they beat off a savage attack by Japanese debouching from the jungle. By the morning of September 1 the way seemed open for a drive to clear the enemy from Milne Bay, as soon as the second battalion of regulars could be brought forward.

Everything seemed propitious; but once again Clowes was

held back by two circumstances: bad weather and uncertainty about Japanese intentions.

Rain continued to pour from low-lying clouds. By September 1 the road to K. B. Mission was impassable. Small boats had to be used to send supplies across the bay from Gili Gili and evacuate the wounded, and small boats were the only means of getting the second battalion of regulars to the front. Nevertheless, the movement was being planned for the second day when Clowes received an order from MacArthur to 'take immediate stations' to repel a land attack from the west on the all-important airfield near Gili Gili. Clowes ordered all units to remain in place all night. No attack occurred.

Not until the morning of September 3 was the second battalion of regulars, shuttled across the bay to K. B. Mission in two small boats, able to begin the offensive. These fresh troops as they moved out were able to overcome a Japanese strongpoint and by nightfall were in perimeter defense a mile east of K. B. Mission. During the next two days the regulars, pressing forward, encountered stiffening resistance as they neared the main Japanese base; on September 5 they were at one point stopped by heavy fire. But with the help of artillery and mortars, and Kittyhawk fighter planes swooping low to strafe the Japanese positions, the Australians kept going.

By nightfall of September 5 the opposition seemed to have melted away. The Australians bivouacked for the night. Enemy ships came into the bay, but did not shell the coast. Around midnight, over the dark water, came the sound of motor boats hurrying between the ships and the shore.

The boats heard that night were in fact evacuating the bulk of the enemy forces. By dawn of September 6 about 1,300 of the men that remained of the 1,900-man invading forces were on their way back to Rabaul. When the Australians resumed their march that morning, they found the main Japanese base deserted; and they met only isolated stragglers.

In one of those coincidences that seem so ironical to a hard-pressed commander, the day the Japanese withdrew was the day General Clowes received his first supplies from Australia since the battle began. On the morning of September 6, the freighter *Anshun* loaded with ammunition and other stores came into Milne Bay, escorted by an Australian warship, and tied up at Gili Gili wharf. Late that afternoon a hospital ship, the *Manunda,* came in to take aboard the sick and wounded soldiers (365 sick and 164 wounded) who had been suffering in sodden tents and native huts. By that time the warship had withdrawn on orders to stay outside the bay during the night.

Around ten o'clock, while the *Anshun* was still unloading by the light of a moon shining fitfully through broken clouds, and the *Manunda* was standing out in the bay, its white and green hull brightly lit in accordance with international law, both ships were suddenly illuminated by the searchlights of two Japanese warships. The hospital ship was spared, but the *Anshun* was shelled and sunk. Her panic-stricken Chinese crew, running up the beach road in the dim moonlight, came very near being mistaken for Japanese invaders; they were recognized just in time.

On the following night the Japanese ships returned and fired on the shores, causing some casualties (but again sparing the hospital ship); and when the skies cleared on September 8, Japanese planes dropped bombs on the bivouac area of the American engineers, killing four men and wounding seven, but the only ground action resulted from encounters with Japanese stragglers attempting to make their way north to Buna.

No further landings occurred. Port Moresby was saved.

In the fourteen-day battle for Milne Bay, 161 Australians were accounted killed or missing in action and one American was killed in ground action. The Japanese dead were about six hundred.

At comparatively small cost, the Australians had beaten off the Japanese invasion forces; indeed, the Battle of Milne Bay was the first time in World War II (except for the initial assault on Wake Island) that a Japanese amphibious operation had been repulsed. The morale value was very great. In far-off Burma, Field Marshal Sir William Slim told his troops that 'of all the Allies it was Australian soldiers who first broke the spell of the invincibility of the Japanese Army.'

Behind the general rejoicing, there were some disturbing reflections at Allied Headquarters in Brisbane. The most serious were in the mind of General MacArthur. Having sent a full brigade of the 7th Division to Milne Bay well ahead of the invasion, he could not understand why Clowes with 4,500 ground troops had not speedily repelled the 1,900 Japanese.

47

General Blamey was also inclined to be critical of Clowes: it seemed 'to us here' – at Brisbane – 'as though, by not acting with great speed,' Clowes had 'missed the opportunity of dealing completely with the enemy.'

Neither MacArthur nor Blamey had seen the terrain. General Rowell after visiting Milne Bay was convinced that Clowes had been right in not leaving his all-important airfield in the west unprotected while the Japanese had control of the bay and could make landings anywhere at any time. If Clowes had been able to move his forces swiftly around the coast to repel attacks, that might have been another matter; but heavy rains clogging the roads made this impossible; and he lacked the boats that would have given him a degree of mobility by water.

Those on the scene could attest to the valor of the untrained Australian militiamen in repelling the first attacks, and could appreciate the bravery and resourcefulness of the regulars in driving the Japanese from the shores.

General MacArthur was inclined to give the credit for the victory to his own foresight in concentrating, unknown to the enemy, superior forces at Milne Bay. He wrote General Marshall: 'The enemy's defeat at Milne Bay must not be accepted as a measure of relative fighting capacity of the troops involved.'

The Australians with some reason considered this comment 'ungenerous'; however, it was made to support an appeal for forces to redress a general situation that was causing MacArthur great anxiety, notably on the Kokoda Track, where the enemy was steadily pushing the defenders back toward Port Moresby.

CHAPTER IV

RETREAT FROM ISURAVA

At dawn on August 27 the Japanese renewed their attack on Isurava. Repulsed on the main track the day before, they had moved around to the jungle on the left, brought up reinforcements, and lain waiting in the dripping darkness for the morning mists to clear.

Awakened by shots, the Australian commander, Lieutenant Colonel Ralph Honner of the 39th Battalion (once a schoolmaster), prepared to 'stand and fight' – orders which he had heard at more than one pass in Greece, 'including famed Thermopylae. At Isurava the green-clad slopes and valleys, the tumbling torrents bright in the morning sunlight, the keen, crisp mountain air' all brought to mind 'the glory that was Greece.' Isurava, he thought, could yet be Australia's Thermopylae.

Reinforcements were beginning to come in. One company of 7th Division regulars of the 21st Brigade had arrived from Myola the afternoon before, wearing shirts and shorts hastily dyed jungle green. The rest of the forward battalion was expected next day, and a second battalion was not far behind. Honner felt the line would hold.

Late that morning he walked with several men to a creek in the rear, for a bath. They were washing and shaving when a runner dashed up and handed Honner a message. Honner turned to one of his company commanders with a grin and said, 'Captain Merritt, when you've finished your shave will you go up to your company. The Japs have broken through your perimeter.' Half-shaved, Merritt was 'off like a race horse'. Later he recalled, 'Honner was the coolest man I've ever seen.'

The attack followed a familiar pattern. First, weird chanting rose in the still air; then, to the accompaniment of the thunder of mortar bombs and mountain-gun shells echoing through the hills, the Japanese erupted from the jungle. Seen close up, in hand-to-hand combat, they seemed surprisingly tall – some were more than six feet – and very formidable. But counterattacks by the Australians with Bren gun and Tommy gun, with bayonet and grenade, and the arrival in the afternoon of another company from Myola, turned the tide. At dusk from the thick undergrowth on the left a bugle rang out, and the Japanese vanished into the jungle.

Next day, in heavy fog, Japanese of 'powerful physique' again attempted, 'wildly screeching', to rush forward positions – but were again beaten back. In the afternoon fresh troops arrived from Myola. With them was their battalion commander, Lieutenant Colonel A. S. Key, a tall, soft-spoken man, who took over from Honner; and they brought with them an effective 3-inch mortar. Its first shot scattered a fire in which the Japanese were cremating their dead.

Our casualties are great, a Japanese officer wrote in his diary on the evening of August 28. *The outcome of the battle is very difficult to foresee.*

In their first two days at the front the Australian veterans of the Middle East had done better than they knew. The Japanese they repulsed were not the advance troops who had pushed the 39th Battalion out of Kokoda, but crack combat troops of Major General Tomitaro Horii's South Seas Detachment.

General Horii, conqueror of Rabaul, remote and impressive to his troops astride his well-groomed white horse, was a small stout gentleman no longer young, with gray hair and spectacles and an air of natural dignity and command. He liked to campaign with his troops and had his headquarters well forward. He was at Kokoda by midafternoon on August 24, planning a speedy advance over the mountains, though (as one of his orders stated) 'it is not certain whether horses can be used.'

He envisaged a march of two days from Kokoda to 'the mountain range' (presumably Myola) and five days from the mountain range to 'MO' (Port Moresby). All that stood in his way, he thought, was the weakened 39th Battalion, in flight after its defeat at Kokoda. Holding Yazawa Force in reserve at Kokoda, he committed only three battalions. Their orders were to take Isurava and go around the Australians' rear to cut them off at Iola. But on August 28, watching the battle from heights less than a mile away, General Horii was becoming impatient. His timetable was being disrupted. Sometime during the night he discovered that the 39th Battalion had been reinforced. He decided to commit his Yazawa Force.

On the morning of August 29 the full crushing weight of the Japanese offensive bore down upon the defenders of Isurava. The Australians fought back in counterattack after counterattack, but by evening Key's position was hopeless, his losses mounting. At dark, just as the clouds parted and moonlight was flickering through the trees, he pulled his men back half a mile up the track. There, next morning, he tried to set up defenses; but soon became aware that the enemy was outflanking his position from high ground on the left and a ravine on the right. He obtained from Brigadier Potts permission to fall back to Alola.

In the withdrawal Key and some of his staff were forced off the track and into the ravine, where they were attacked by a Japanese patrol and had to scatter into the jungle. Ten days later Key and four of his men were captured. In October the Japanese brought into their base near Buna a prisoner that Father Benson described at a tall, gaunt Australian with the star and crown of a lieutenant colonel on his shoulder tab. He had a nasty leg wound and was 'an emaciated skeleton'. He was sent to Rabaul, and nothing more was heard of him.

Most of Key's forces fought their way back to Alola, but when the Japanese moved in strength across the track on the afternoon of August 30, they cut off more than forty men who had remained behind to bring out the wounded. This party, led by twenty-three-year-old Captain S. H. Buckler, had to leave the track. Burdened with clumsy stretchers and moving at the pace of the walking wounded, one of whom had a shattered leg and was crawling on his hands and knees, Buckler and his men set out into the dark jungle country to the east on a month-long journey of terrible hardships.

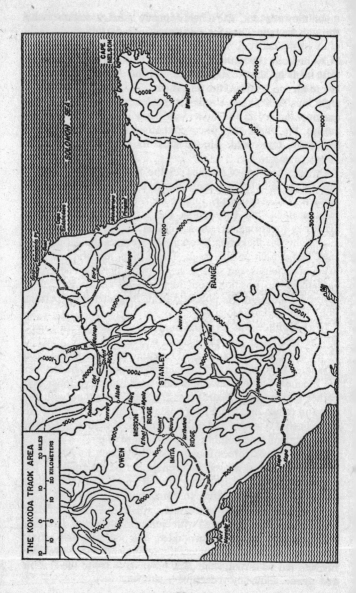

THE KOKODA TRACK AREA

As they set out, they heard heavy gunfire reverberating through the hills. The Japanese were shelling Alola.

Potts ordered the withdrawal of Maroubra Force to the next settlement up the Kokoda Track, Eora Creek Village. As the last of his men climbed the hill above Alola, the sudden tropical night was falling, but there was still light enough to see the enemy entering the village and feasting on the rations left behind. The Japanese raised their flag, their brilliant red rising sun, over Alola, and beneath it held a victory parade. The Australians watched it in the fading daylight, then started up the track.

At dusk they encountered the first war correspondents to reach the front. Correspondent Osmar White and photographer Damien Parer were told that it was no use going forward, and turned back with the troops.

Night was falling and the 'six o'clock crickets' set up their shrilling. Then the evening rains came down. All night in the pouring rain and soupy mud, Osmar White passed long lines of wounded men, some of whom ought to have been on stretchers if there had been bearers enough. One man whose leg had been blown off below the knee, the stump dressed and wrapped in an old copra sack, crawled and hopped along. Some lay exhausted beside the path: one was a black shape on a pile of glowing phosphorescent fungus, looking as if he were lying on a pyre of heatless embers.

Now and then a voice in the pitch-black dark appealed to White, 'Dig, I say Dig, are you going to Eora? Tell them to send a light down the trail, will you? Tell them to send a light, Dig.' Lacking a light to guide them, each man held onto the man ahead.

All night and all the next day the track to Eora Creek Village was congested with wounded men, fleeing native carriers, and Maroubra Force in retreat.

'An army in retreat,' said Damien Parer to White. 'Not a very pretty sight, is it?'

The men's clothing was sodden and ragged, their wide-brimmed felt hats mud-spattered and rain-soaked, their steel helmets red with rust, their unshaven faces pallid under mud and grime. They moved slowly, carrying their wounded on stretchers up steep slopes and over slippery logs spanning rushing waters.

By dusk on August 31, Brigadier Potts and his vanguard of regulars were passing through Eora Creek Village, a cluster of thatched-roofed huts foundering in the mud on a shelf of the V-shaped cleft made by the creek, and by nightfall were in position on the heights above. There Potts received a message from the commander of the 7th Division, Major General Arthur S. Allen, ordering him to hold where he was; Allen, a plump, amiable general nicknamed 'Tubby', added, 'Keep smiling.'

Potts knew that he could not hold. He was down to fewer than 600 regulars. Honner's 39th Battalion, almost finished as a fighting unit but gallantly assisting the rearguard battalion of regulars to cover the retreat, had orders to return to Port Moresby. The Japanese were in steady pursuit. Patrols saw them advancing on both flanks, their engineers clearing tracks and building shelters, covered with palm leaves, in which they stored dry wood. But though the Japanese were in sight, they were out of range of Australian weapons. Potts called for air strikes, but nothing happened. He decided to fall back to his base at Myola.

With this news, the war correspondents immediately set out for Port Moresby. Osmar White returned with deep misgivings about the fighting on the Kokoda Track. He had observed how the soldiers clung to the track, which they considered their life line. They did not know how to live in the jungle – the art of 'bushcraft'; moreover, they had been told by their officers that if they held the Kokoda Track they would hold the Owen Stanley Range, 'the natural defense line,' according to General MacArthur (who had never seen it), guarding Port Moresby. White, who had covered Australian guerrilla operations in the mountains near Lae, saw that the important thing was not the track, but high ground. The Japanese, trained jungle fighters, were able to outflank track positions by climbing to heights on either side.

In the pullback to Myola beginning September 2, the Japanese advance troops outflanked Potts's rearguard battalion at dusk and forced it off the track. All night and most of the next day the men of the rear guard tore their way through the thick jungle underbrush, tortured by hunger and so thirsty that they sucked water from the moss on the trees. Making a wide encircling movement they got back on the track in the afternoon, catching up with Potts, who ordered them to continue covering the retreat.

When the weary, rain-soaked men of the vanguard stumbled into Myola late on the night of September 3, they found waiting for them at the cookhouse a hot stew of bully beef, rice, dried vegetables, and biscuits. In the jungle fringing the clearing, huts thatched with palm leaves sheltered ample supplies. Next morning Potts's men had a bath in the creek that ran through the clearing and were issued fresh clothing to replace the sodden, filthy shirts and shorts they had worn since they left Port Moresby. For more than a week they had not been able to take off their shoes: from swollen, pulpy feet the socks had to be cut away.

While the men rested next morning, exposing their swollen feet to the sun, Potts, who had received a message from General Allen stressing the 'vital necessity' of holding Myola, set out with a reconnaissance party to study the terrain. Climbing a mountain spur they saw beyond the base a second and larger dry lake bed, the rippling kunai grass stretching almost as far as the eye could see.

The defense of this vast area was clearly impossible with the small force at hand. Potts had been told by Allen that another brigade of the 7th Division, the 25th, was on its way to Port Moresby, and he had learned that advance companies of his own reserve battalion were nearing Myola; but as the afternoon wore on, it became plain that none of these reinforcements could arrive in time. A runner dashed in with the news that the Japanese had again broken through the rear guard and were in hot pursuit.

Potts ordered a withdrawal to Efogi, the next mountain spur to the rear. At nightfall, all the supplies at Myola that could not be carried on the retreat were destroyed, including some 10,000 rations and 41,000 rounds of ammunition. At first light on September 5, when the rear guard arrived, the storage huts were fired. When the last of the Australians departed from Myola that morning they left behind a desolate clearing carpeted with muddy, rain-soaked rice and strewn with ration tins punctured so that the food would spoil.

Passing through Efogi Village next day, and climbing to

the heights above, known as Mission Ridge, Potts's men were cheered to see in position new arrivals from Port Moresby, the fresh troops of the brigade's reserve battalion. 'By hell,' they said, 'we're glad to see you blokes here.'

Potts set up his headquarters in a roofless shack surrounded by kunai grass on the crest of Mission Ridge.

Through the kunai grass in the burning heat of midafternoon, a party of soldiers brought bad news. The remnants of a patrol that had been badly crippled by enemy fire, they reported that the Japanese had passed through Myola and were moving down the track toward Efogi. The crucial Battle of Efogi was about to begin.

Late in the afternoon, troops on the perimeter, scanning Efogi Village through binoculars, saw hundreds of Japanese soldiers sitting around the village huts eating from their mess tins. After nightfall the Australians on the heights above saw a procession of lights moving down the track on the hillside across from them – Japanese soldiers carrying lanterns – and got as much amusement as they could when they saw the lanterns bobbing up and down or flying off the track when their owners slipped in the mud or stumbled on roots. But as the procession continued, for most of the night, the brigade staff watched grim-faced. Though Potts was in a commanding position on the heights, he did not have weapons with long enough range to stop the enemy. There was one other resource. He sent off a message to New Guinea Force requesting an air strike on Efogi at first light.

At dawn the planes appeared, bombers and fighters flying almost level with the spur, then diving to the attack on Efogi Village. The thunder and flash of the explosions, the debris of thatched huts flying upward through the smoke, delighted the watchers on the heights; but the planes were unable to stop the Japanese, protected as they were by the thick jungle. Half an hour after the first air attack, they were seen reconnoitering an old mission hut only 300 yards below the Australians' perimeter in the tall kunai grass near the top of the ridge.

The men on the perimeter spent a miserable day. The sun beat down on the kunai, which offered no shade. During the afternoon their water bottles ran dry. Rations were running low.

Night fell and a small new moon rose over the ridges toward Myola. By its faint light the Australians buried their dead. When they looked across at the hills beyond Efogi, they saw great fires where the Japanese were cremating their own dead.

During the day General Horii set up his headquarters at Efogi. He had just been considerably reinforced. On the night of September 2–3 the third battalion of Colonel Kiyomi Yazawa's 41st Regiment had landed near Gona and set out at once over the mountains to join Yazawa Force. These reinforcements brought Horii's strength to about 5,000 fighting men, supported by engineers, service troops, and two mountain guns. Determined to take Mission Ridge without further delay, he ordered elements of four battalions to attack on the hilltop and flanks at dawn. At the same time a machine-gun company was to encircle the Australian positions from the rear, isolating them.

The small moon was still visible in the early morning darkness of September 8 when Australian sentries heard noises in the jungle below and alerted the men on the perimeter. At five o'clock there was a hail of small arms fire and at first light, mortar and mountain-gun fire raked the area. Shortly after dawn Potts's headquarters was fired upon by a party of Japanese working around the flanks. The headquarters men – Potts himself and even the cook – fired back at ranges as short as 15 yards. A party sent from the front lines to extricate him was cut to pieces; and soon no more help could reach him, because during the day the Japanese moved in strength across the track between the headquarters position and the perimeter. As night fell, Potts was able to make his way back to the next staging area, Menari. By then the men on the perimeter had left the track and plunged into the jungle.

Survivors of the two most experienced battalions, those who had come down the track from Isurava, managed next day to find their way to Menari; but no stand was possible there. By afternoon Japanese patrols were appearing, some of them dressed in uniforms stripped from the Australian dead, and Menari was being bombarded. The retreat continued.

By September 11 the 21st Brigade, now down to little more than three hundred men, was at Ioribaiwa Ridge, only a short distance north of Port Moresby's last bastion – Imita Ridge. These troops were now so close to the town that when the wind was right they could hear the drone of airplane motors from its airfields. They were ordered to hold until relief came. Beating off Japanese probing attacks, they were holding two days later when the 25th Brigade began arriving.

The fresh brigade, the first troops to be outfitted in 'jungle green' uniforms with long trousers, was commanded by Brigadier Kenneth W. Eather, a capable, energetic leader aged forty-one. Taking over command in the forward area (Potts had been relieved a few days earlier), he immediately began an offensive to regain control of the track as far as Kokoda.

He planned a pincers movement toward his first objective, Nauro, a vital airdropping area on the track between Ioribaiwa and Menari. Ordering the weary remnants of the 21st Brigade, astride the track in the most forward position at Ioribaiwa, to hold, and placing one of his fresh battalions behind them, he ordered two of his 25th Brigade battalions forward in a flanking movement around the Ioribaiwa position, one to make a wide encircling advance on the right, the other to climb to high ground on the left and take Nauro. The latter was to make the first move, on September 14.

Things did not go according to plan. When the left battalion swung off the track on a narrow ridge, it came under Japanese fire sited on higher ground and was stopped. Next day the battalion on the right also failed to dislodge the enemy; and the forward position at Ioribaiwa came under heavy, costly, machine-gun and mortar fire from Japanese dug in nearby.

The following morning the Japanese attacked furiously on left, center, and right, the heaviest fire falling where it would have the most effect, on the battle-weary men of the 21st Brigade. They were beginning to crack up. One fainted when assisting at the burial of a comrade; others wept openly. All were demoralized, resenting having to bear the brunt of the battle in the forward position, while fresh troops were in their rear.

Brigadier Eather, usually imperturbable, was shaken by the situation erupting around him. He asked permission to withdraw to Imita Ridge.

Over the weak, sputtering telephone line to Port Moresby he said to General Allen: 'I want your permission to withdraw, Chief. I know what I'm doing. I must have a firm base for the start of my offensive, and it doesn't exist here.'

Allen gave Eather permission to make the decision on whether or not to pull back, but added, 'There won't be any withdrawal from the Imita position, Ken. You'll die there if necessary. You understand that?'

When General Rowell was told of this conversation, he said to Allen, 'Our heads will be in the basket over this, Tubby.' But he gave his approval.

Eather decided to pull back. By noon next day, September 17, he was setting up his position on Imita Ridge.

The small group of survivors of the 21st Brigade were on their way to the rear. These men bore little resemblance to the cheerful, bronzed Middle East veterans who in mid-August had started so confidently over the Kokoda Track. Their faces had a waxy pallor; their shirts of faded khaki-green, caked with mud, hung from bony shoulders.

While they were resting and refitting at Port Moresby, they were rejoined by several parties that had been cut off in the Owen Stanleys and forced to disappear into the jungle to avoid capture, painfully making their way southward through the steaming undergrowth and living on yams and taro from native gardens.

Perhaps the most remarkable story was told by young Captain Buckler, who on the evening of August 30 had led his party off the track between Isurava and Alola. Finding the Japanese in possession at Alola, he had plunged with his men into the wilderness, moving eastward toward the coastal plain, where the weather was warmer and the chances better of obtaining native food.

At a native village between Kokoda and the Kumusi River crossing at Wairopi, he left six wounded men with a medical orderly and with those still able to walk he went east to Wairopi, then south up the swift Kumusi River over a little-used native track leading through Jaure over very high mountains to the coast east of Port Moresby. Anxious to get help quickly for the wounded men he had left behind, young Captain Buckler pushed on alone ahead of his party, guided by a native boy. After he passed Jaure he came to the summit of the range – 'Ghost Mountain', a mist-shrouded 9,100-foot peak 2,000 feet higher than anything on the Kokoda Track, a place of icy winds and silent moss forests, shunned by the natives as being haunted.

Coming down from these eerie heights on the morning of September 28, Buckler beheld a sight that seemed almost a mirage. Beside the track sat eight soldiers whose deep, bucket-like helmets and long trousers proclaimed them to be Americans.

CHAPTER V

"MUST I ALWAYS LEAD A FORLORN HOPE?"

On their part the Americans gazed at Buckler as if he were an apparition. They had been told that no white man had passed over the divide since 1917.

Their own presence on these remote, mist-shrouded heights was the result of General MacArthur's consternation when he learned that the Australians had been driven out of Myola on September 5. He immediately dispatched to Port Moresby his trusted Chief of Staff, General Sutherland, his 'eyes and ears', to bring back reliable, firsthand information on the reason why.

Sutherland returned with the information that the Australians had been badly outnumbered, and that General Rowell was sure they could regain the initiative with the help of the 25th Brigade. Moreover, the 25th would soon be joined by a third brigade, the 16th, trained jungle fighters recently arrived in Australia from Ceylon. MacArthur was satisfied, and began to plan 'a wide turning movement' over the mountains east of the Kokoda Track, to cut in on the enemy's rear.

He planned to use American combat troops – the first to be sent to New Guinea. The two U.S. infantry divisions that had arrived by ship in Australia in the late spring, the 32d and 41st, were then in training on the east coast and had just been combined into I Corps. MacArthur considered that a regiment taken from one or the other of these two divisions would be sufficient to make his 'wide turning movement', and he left the choice of the unit to the newly arrived commander of I Corps, Major General Robert L. Eichelberger, a tall, thin, black-browed, gray-haired man of fifty-six who had been secretary of the General Staff of the U.S. Army when MacArthur was Chief of Staff, and was later superintendent of West Point.

Eichelberger knew next to nothing about jungle warfare, and after an inspection of his troops he came to the conclusion that the two American divisions knew little more. Almost at random he decided to take a regiment from the 32d Division. Composed mainly of National Guardsmen from Michigan and Wisconsin, the division had a great deal of *esprit de corps*, proud of the name it had won in World War I, 'Les Terribles'. Its commander, Major General Edwin F. Harding, had been a classmate of Eichelberger's at West Point and was also fifty-six years old, but looked younger, a small, dark-haired man with a handsome, resolute, face and a confident manner. On Harding's recommendation, Eichelberger selected the U.S. 32d's 126th Infantry Regiment to make the flanking movement over the mountains on the east.

To MacArthur's planners, an advance over these eastern mountains appeared to have some advantages over the Kokoda Track. It could be supplied more easily from Port Moresby, partly by a coastal road and partly by sea, to a point on the coast near the village of Kapa Kapa where the track began and from which it came to be known as the Kapa Kapa Track. From Kapa Kapa a road of sorts to a rubber plantation at Kalikodobu (which the Americans rechristened Kalamazoo) would be widened and improved. As the track climbed to the dizzying heights of the 'Ghost Mountain' area, airdrops would have to be depended upon. But after about 16 miles of mountain crest, the track dropped to Jaure, at the headwaters of the Kumusi River, and from there two tracks offered great possibilities. One of them cut in behind the Japanese at the Kumusi River crossing (Wairopi) – the Japanese life-line between Kokoda and the Japanese supply dumps on the coast. The other track went east over the coastal plain to Buna.

Thus the Kapa Kapa Track appeared on the map. But the hardships of the climb over the virtually unexplored heights were either unperceived at MacArthur's headquarters or dismissed as negligible; and the men who were to suffer them were woefully unprepared.

On the afternoon of September 15, Company E of the 126th U.S. Infantry Regiment came into Port Moresby by air, its mission to pave the way for the rest of the regiment, which was to take ship at Brisbane a few days later. Nearly all of the men of the company came from Grand Rapids, Michigan, and for most of them it was their first travel by air.

When they disembarked from their transports at Seven Mile Airdrome, their fatigues still wet from the mottled green, brown, and yellow 'jungle dye' hastily applied the night before by a Brisbane dry cleaning firm, they were greeted by cheers from the men working around the airfield. *Japs twenty miles away,* wrote Company E's top sergeant in his notebook. This was an exaggeration, but was written down as a fact, along with the notation that *New Guinea weather is hotter than the lower story of hell.*

Early next morning Company E was sent eastward to start building the road to Kapa Kapa. The steaming coast was even hotter than Port Moresby. The Americans soon discarded their helmets for the Army's cloth 'fisherman's hat'; and this continued to be the Americans' favorite head covering under the broiling tropical sun of the New Guinea coast. The newcomers kept a sharp lookout for Japanese patrols. No Japanese appeared, but the strange sights and sounds of the jungle kept the men jumpy. One night three soldiers on patrol were awakened by the barking of a dog, followed by a rustle of leaves, a snap and a crunch, then silence. At daylight they saw huge crocodile tracks ten feet away. While the men were building the road (it took five days), a reconnaissance party, headed by the regimental intelligence officer, began to climb the Kapa Kapa Track. These were the men that Buckler encountered.

The Americans had hardly begun building the coastal road in preparation for MacArthur's optimistic flanking movement when bad news from New Guinea arrived like a thunderclap at MacArthur's headquarters in Brisbane. The Australians on the Kokoda Track – even after reinforcement by the 25th Brigade – had on September 17 withdrawn from Ioribaiwa to Imita Ridge.

That evening General MacArthur called Australian Prime Minister John Curtin on the 'secraphone' from Brisbane to Sydney. He informed Curtin that the Australians, though they now outnumbered the Japanese in the Owen Stanleys (he was

63

convinced of this), were still withdrawing. The reason could only be that the troops were not efficient. He admitted that the Australian military leaders, including General Blamey, were confident that the Japanese could be held. MacArthur did not share their confidence. He felt that, if the Japanese penetration continued, 'the Allies in New Guinea would be forced into such a defensive concentration as would duplicate the conditions of Malaya." He did not have adequate naval support and he thought the American position in the Solomons was unfavorable.

These were his words to Curtin. Behind them was the mood of despair that sometimes overwhelmed him, expressed on one occasion in a bitter outcry, 'Must I always lead a forlorn hope?'

To keep New Guinea from being 'stitched into the Japanese pattern of quick conquest', he intended, he told Curtin, to send American troops by air and sea to stem the attack. Within a week he expected to have 40,000 men in New Guinea, 'and if they fought, they should have no trouble in meeting the situation. If they would not fight, 100,000 there would be no good.' And he requested that General Blamey be sent at once to New Guinea to take command and 'energize the situation'.

Orders had already gone out to the Americans. The 32d Division's 126th Regiment was in Brisbane ready to take ship for New Guinea the following morning. The division's 128th Regiment was moving by train and plane from its camp near Brisbane to the airfield at Townsville to fly to Port Moresby, using transport planes, civilian as well as military, rounded up by General Kenney from all over Australia. This was the first mass troop movement by air in World War II. By September 23 the transports were disembarking the last elements of the 128th at Seven Mile Airdrome.

That same afternoon, General Blamey also arrived in Port Moresby.

He was coldly received by General Rowell, who considered the visit to be strong evidence that Blamey had lost confidence in him. Between the two men there were striking personal contrasts. Blamey (in peacetime a police chief) with his white mustache and paunch looked incongruous in his khaki shirt and shorts; his plump knees, revealed by his shorts, inspired the war correspondents to refer to him among themselves as 'Dimple-knees'. His wide-brimmed felt hat was usually worn on the back of his head. Rowell, ten years younger, was handsome and soldierly. He had great pride in his profession, and was touchy at interference.

At the moment he was particularly sensitive to any proposal that would draw strength away from the Kokoda Track. He considered MacArthur's 'flank operation' unsound. He was also very skeptical of a recent proposal by MacArthur's headquarters to create a landing field on the coast south of Buna. This was a project fostered by General Kenney, who had been told by an Australian pilot of a feasible landing place – level ground covered by kunai grass – at the base of Cape Nelson near Wanigela, an old Anglican mission, considerably more than halfway up the 170-mile stretch of coast that ran from Milne Bay to Buna. Kenney flew over it, considered it 'a natural', and talked it up to General MacArthur.

In Rowell's eyes, the 'Wanigela concept' was 'all of a pattern with the American idea of outflanking the mountains'. He told Blamey it would only lead to the Japanese landing more troops at Buna. Nevertheless, Blamey, on the second day after his arrival in New Guinea, flew over Wanigela Mission, liked it, and arranged with General Clowes to send a battalion of Australian troops by air from Milne Bay to prepare the airfield.

This action, taken without consulting Rowell, brought on an acrimonious exchange between the two men that led to Rowell's relief on the morning of September 28. As his successor Blamey named Lieutenant General Edmund F. Herring, a 'small and quiet man' who had a talent for diplomacy.

In one of the ironies so common in war, Rowell had hardly departed when the situation on the Kokoda Track took a dramatic turn for the better.

For ten days, since September 17, the Australians had been on Imita Ridge, only three miles across a deep valley from Ioribaiwa where (patrols reported) the Japanese were strongly entrenched. But the Japanese had not attacked. Even after a bombardment by heavy artillery manhandled to the heights by Australian soldiers, they remained strangely passive.

On September 27 the Australians began to move on Ioribaiwa. Closing in at nightfall, the center battalion came up against elaborate fortifications. Across the track was a fence made of tree trunks. Next morning when the attack was resumed, Eather's men found a connecting network of weapon pits and command posts spread out fanwise from the village of Ioribaiwa.

All were empty. The Japanese had withdrawn. It was obviously a planned retreat: they had taken their weapons and equipment. At General Horii's command post were found only a cane chair, bags of books, and a quantity of white gloves.

The jubilant Australians believed that exhaustion and hunger had defeated the enemy; that the hardships of their own mountain campaign were now operating, even more effectively, against the Japanese.

In fact, the Japanese had withdrawn on orders from Tokyo.

It was true that many of Horii's soldiers were suffering from wounds, malaria, malnutrition, and pneumonia. Their uniforms were stained with mud and blood. But when they stood on the rocky summit at Ioribaiwa they were 'wild with joy', reported Seizo Okada, a war correspondent accompanying them. Rejoicing that 'the endless waves of mountains upon mountains' that had 'wearied' their eyes had 'suddenly vanished', they saw through the trees a wide expanse of forest gradually sloping to the foothills, and beyond that a sheet of light.

'The sea!' cried the soldiers, weeping and throwing themselves into one another's arms, 'Look! It's the sea of Port Moresby!' All through their long march, walled in by enormous mountains, creeping through the eerie, dusky jungle on soft moss-covered ground that made them feel as if they were 'treading on some living animal', they had pressed on, wet to the skin from drumming rains, starving, fighting, dying 'with only one objective in view, asleep or awake – Port Moresby.'

They were not ordered forward immediately. A halt on Ioribaiwa was a part of plans, made before Horii's departure from Rabaul, for a two-pronged advance on Port Moresby by land and sea. The timing was thrown off by the repulse at Milne Bay; nevertheless, preparations went forward for a seaborne force to make an amphibious landing at Port Moresby after Horii reached Ioribaiwa (tentative date for this was mid-October); then the two forces were to attack simultaneously.

Arriving ahead of schedule, Horii began at once to build strong fortifications, to clear fields of fire, and to site his guns. Waiting within this defense position, he counted on his men regaining their strength. To supplement their meager rations, he ordered detachments to gather sugar cane, taro, and vegetables from native gardens; and sent parties over the mountains to bring back provisions from dumps in the rear.

But the meagerness of the supplies that came in was disturbing. Also, bad news came from Guadalcanal, where in mid-September the U.S. Marines defeated a strong Japanese force. According to Seizo Okada: 'An atmosphere of uneasiness stole over the positions on the mountain like the fog that gathered noiselessly every morning.'

On the night of September 24, Okada and a fellow correspondent, sitting in their thatched hut finishing their scanty dinner of sweet potatoes, were visited by a radio operator with startling news. A wireless message had come in from Rabaul ordering General Horii to withdraw to some point in the Owen Stanley Range, leaving to him the choice of the best position.

The two newspapermen hurried to General Horii's tent, which stood on a little hill. As they entered, in the profound stillness of the mountains they saw a dramatic scene, illuminated by the dim light of a candle that cast two shadows on the dirty wet canvas of the tent. One was that of General Horii, sitting upright on his heels on a thin straw mat, his face emaciated, his gray head bare. Opposite him on a mat was his Chief Staff Officer, Lieutenant Colonel Toyanari Tanaka.

The silence was broken by an outburst from Horii: 'I'm not going back, not a step! Are you going back, Tanaka? How can we abandon this position, after all the blood the soldiers have shed and the hardships they have endured? I cannot give such an order.'

Grasping the samurai sword that lay beside him, he added bitterly, 'I will not retreat an inch. I'd rather disguise myself as a native of these mountains and stay here!'

Tamaka was silent, staring at the flame of the candle, avoiding his commander's eyes. Then a rustling sound was heard in the thicket outside and a signalman came in with another message from Rabaul, this time ordering Horii to withdraw completely from the Owen Stanley Range and concentrate on the coast at Buna. Almost immediately a similar order came from the Imperial General Headquarters in Tokyo.

The Japanese planning staffs had somehow gotten wind of General MacArthur's preparations to take Buna and assumed that he had landing craft, like those used by the Americans in the Solomons, to make an amphibious attack. They also believed that MacArthur intended to use paratroops. Horii's orders stated that the Yazawa Force would proceed immediately to Buna and defeat 'the enemy's disembarkation plans, and hold the airfield.'

All night, in a soft drizzle, the Japanese prepared to withdraw from Ioribaiwa. Hot-blooded battalion commanders rebelled, urging a desperate, single-handed thrust into Port Moresby; artillerymen swore they would not leave their guns. Nevertheless, by dawn on September 25 the withdrawal over the mountains had begun.

To cover the withdrawal and gain time for the evacuation of Kokoda, General Horii created a new unit, the Stanley Shitai, consisting of a battalion with supporting engineers and artillery. It was ordered to hold at the deep ravine beyond Myola – the most treacherous spot on the whole Kokoda Track, where Eora Creek roared at the foot of cavernous rocks, the place where Australian troops had been forced off the track in the retreat from Isurava.

The troops of the Stanley Shitai moved out of Myola early in October, following the track leading downward into the ravine through thick bamboo grass that glistened like wet paint, the branches so interwoven that no sunlight could get through. In the pale twilight at the bottom of the ravine they made their way around rotting, maggot-eaten corpses of the September fighting. Then the Japanese climbed to the heights on either side of the ravine, dug weapon pits, sited their guns, and waited.

The Australians moving out of Ioribaiwa up the Kokoda Track on October 1 encountered no Japanese, only evidences of a hasty withdrawal, and pressed on toward Myola. At Efogi they left parties to bury the men killed in the battle at Mission Ridge, about two hundred bodies, Australian and Japanese, lying in a confusion of blood-stained gear. Below the ridge in the bed of Efogi Creek lay the remains of General Horii's white horse. On the track beyond Efogi they saw skeletons picked clean by ants. They also found indications that the retreating Japanese were threatened by starvation; native gardens had been dug up inch by inch; bodies were found without a trace of wounds, and there were signs that the enemy had been eating grass and even wood.

Australian patrols entered Myola before the end of the first week in October and found it abandoned. Then some of the enemy's carriers, natives of Rabaul who had deserted, came out of the jungle and said that the Japanese had fallen back to Kokoda. Optimism grew. General Blamey reported to General MacArthur that the 25th Brigade, followed by the 16th Brigade, was 'pushing forward steadily', and 'we may not have a great deal of trouble to get to Kokoda'.

In Brisbane, the slender, ascetic-looking Deputy Chief of the Australian General Staff, Major General George A. Vasey (known as 'Bloody George' from his fondness for the Australian army's favorite swear word), observed that MacArthur's headquarters was 'like a bloody barometer in a cyclone – up and down every two minutes'.

After the news of the Japanese withdrawal from Ioribaiwa the barometer went up.

On October 1, General MacArthur ordered an all-out attack by New Guinea Force, with two objectives. The first, to be accomplished by simultaneous mountain advances over the Kokoda Track and the Kapa Kapa Track, was to cut off Horii's forces beyond Kokoda at the Kumusi River, thus blocking his withdrawal to Buna. The second objective was to deny to the Japanese the coast of New Guinea from Milne Bay to Cape Nelson, jutting north of Wanigela. The coast was to be occupied and held. Upon securing the line of the Kumusi and the Cape Nelson area, all land forces were to prepare to take Buna.

CHAPTER VI

THE AMERICAN ADVANCE
BY MOUNTAIN AND SEA

Late on the afternoon of October 2, Lewis Sebring of the New York *Herald Tribune* landed at Port Moresby with a planeload of U.S. 32d Division officers and found that he had arrived just in time to cover a historic event: General MacArthur's first visit to New Guinea.

Near the thatched roof of the control tower of Seven Mile Airdrome in the swirling dust and blinding heat stood General Blamey in his shorts and the Australian Minister for the Army, the Right Honorable F. M. Forde, in a huge sun helmet. Milling about these dignitaries was a crowd of American and Australian war correspondents in shapeless khaki dark with sweat. They told Sebring, to his astonishment (for he had heard nothing of it in Brisbane), that General MacArthur was expected at 6.30.

Soon, over the low brown hills, a B-17 bomber appeared. It landed exactly at 6.30. General MacArthur stepped down, wearing his gold-embroidered cap and regulation Army suntan shirt and trousers, his tie hanging outside the shirt, Marine style, instead of tucked in, Army style. His tan shoes had a high polish, which soon disappeared in the dust.

Turning to his pilot, Major Henry C. Godman, he said, 'Nice work, Godman – pretty hard trip for an old man.' Then he was followed from the plane by his two most trusted advisers – General Sutherland and General Kenney, and his public relations officer, Colonel LeGrande A. Diller.

After the picture-taking was over, Diller and Sebring accompanied the newspapermen to the cottage they shared in Port Moresby, a flimsy plasterboard four-room cottage with a veranda on which cots draped with mosquito nets had been set out to accommodate more than a dozen Australian, British, and American correspondents and cameramen. All were suffering from the heat, the clouds of mosquitoes and flies, and the monotonous Australian Army diet of corned beef, beans, crackers, and tea.

The Americans were also suffering from the iron hand of censorship. They had a great story – the arrival of American combat troops in New Guinea, but they were forbidden to report it. The correspondent most frustrated was Byron Darnton of the New York *Times*. A big man of forty-five with a black mustache, always called Barney, and a great favorite with everyone, he had served with the 32d Division in World War I and had hoped to cover it with glory in World War II.

After dinner Colonel Diller told the Americans that General MacArthur was to make an inspection trip 'as far as he could go into the Owen Stanley Range'; and next morning they set out to accompany him, their jeeps following the staff car in which MacArthur was riding, accompanied by General Blamey.

As the roads became worse, the generals transferred from their staff car to a jeep, and soon MacArthur's freshly pressed uniform was spattered with red mud and he was so busy holding onto the jeep that he could only smile, not wave, at the gaunt, weary Australian soldiers coming down the road from the front, staring, stopping to lean on their rifles, the sweat rolling down under their steel helmets.

At a forward supply point piled high with cases of ammunition and rations, MacArthur got out and walked up the road. The correspondents crowded around, asking what he thought of the terrain. The general, fingering an unlighted cigar, said he was reminded of Baguio in the Philippines; the battleground was quite different from Bataan.

'It's a funny thing,' he said. 'Here we are in a new campaign talking about an old one.' He stopped for a moment in deep thought, then went on, 'The bitterness of such a campaign can only be realized by those who have gone through it. Robert E. Lee was the last great captain that led a lost cause. But this is different. His was permanently lost; mine only temporarily.'

These words, thought Sebring, revealed 'the real MacArthur.

71

He conceived himself to be a "great captain" leading a great cause.' His statement was genuine, it was from the heart. 'He really believed it; he certainly had the admirable quality of supreme confidence in himself.' Some might call it supreme vanity – 'but that was, and continued to be, MacArthur.'

Near the place where the heavy artillery had been emplaced to fire on Ioribaiwa, MacArthur's party came upon a battalion of the Australian 16th Brigade on its way to the front. To its commander, Brigadier J. E. Lloyd, MacArthur said, 'Lloyd, by some act of God, your brigade has been chosen for this job. The eyes of the western world are upon you. I have every confidence in you and your men. Good luck and don't stop.'

The general's caravan continued over a road even more primitive, a succession of deep downward and upward pitches, until it reached the end of the jeep road, a flat place where supplies were let down by pulleys several hundred feet into a gorge. There the narrow red Kokoda Track began, descending into a green valley hidden by jungle growth. Across the valley rose the first of the big green mountains of the Owen Stanley Range.

General MacArthur got out of his jeep and walked to the edge of the gorge to look at the mountain beyond. Then he went into a supply tent labeled 'The Flying Fox', where an Australian army cook who called himself 'Gestapo Gus' served him a cup of coffee and got his autograph. The notables posed for pictures and set out on the return journey. Early next morning MacArthur and his party took off for Australia.

Two days later, on October 6, the vanguard of the first – and only – American force to climb the Owen Stanley mountains started up the Kapa Kapa Track. An encouraging report had just come into General Harding from the commander of the eight-man reconnaissance party (the one encountered by Captain Buckler): the Kapa Kapa Track was 'practicable for marching', even though it was 'taxing'.

In fact, the ascent was to be far more arduous than anything the Australians had experienced on the Kokoda Track.

Moreover, the men of the vanguard had not yet become acclimated and knew little about mountain climbing. They were the Antitank and Cannon Companies (250 men, supported by a hundred native carriers) of the 126th Infantry's 2d Battalion, called Mendendorp Force from their commander, Captain Alfred Mendendorp. The battalion's Company E had been roadbuilding in the Kapa Kapa area for three weeks; but these men had only recently arrived by ship from Australia.

The first day's march of 14 miles from 'Kalamazoo' to Nepeana ought to have been easy, because Company E had built a jeep road as far as Nepeana, but it was not. The grades on the road were so steep that jeeps sometimes had to take several runnings starts before they could get to the top of the hills. At the end of the first day the men were already exhausted.

Two days out of Nepeana, Mendendorp Force reached the foothills of the Owen Stanley Range. The grades became ever steeper and the footing more slippery. As Captain Mendendorp described the third day's march,

Leeches and insects began to be a nuisance. The trail was strewn with cast-off articles. Leather toilet sets, soap, socks, and extra underwear told a tale of exhaustion and misery. Upon reaching streams, the men would rush to them and drink, regardless of the fact that upstream some soldier might be washing his feet. The trail was filled with struggling individuals, many lying on one side panting for breath. The medical officer bringing up the rear, reached the bivouac that night with a platoon of limping and dazed men. There were no stragglers, however, for it was feared all through the march that stragglers might be killed by a Jap patrol.

Their nerves on edge, the men were badly shaken by an occurrence the following night. Down the dark track that led into their bivouac from the heights ahead there staggered a party of thirty-five gaunt, emaciated Australian soldiers caked with blood and so pale they looked like ghosts. They were the men who had followed Captain Buckler over the mountains. These apparitions coming down from Ghost Mountain frightened the native carriers. Next day most of them deserted, and Mendendorp Force had to carry its own supplies on the hard climb to the mountaintop at Laruni.

Leaving behind a detachment to take care of the air-dropping ground planned at Laruni, Mendendorp pushed on with his main force up the Owen Stanley divide, a region of icy heights and strange forests where trees were covered with moss six inches thick. No birds sang and there was perpetual twilight.

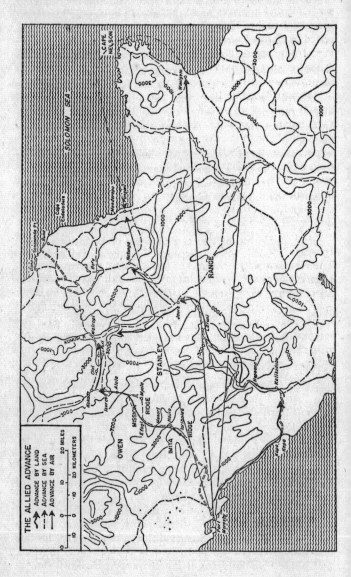

Here the track was so narrow that the troops had to walk single file and in places was so rough that they had to crawl on hands and knees. When they were too exhausted to go on, they rested by simply leaning forward, clinging to vines and roots to keep from slipping down the mountainside. Edging along cliff walls, hanging onto vines, they could only with great effort do more than two miles a day.

Not until October 20 were the men of Mendendorp Force able to reach Jaure on the far side of the divide. It had taken them nearly a week to cross the 16 miles of the divide.

As punishing as the march was for the vanguard, it was even worse for the main body of the 2d Battalion, a force almost 900 strong (including the Company E roadbuilders), supported by several hundred native carriers. The day after this force set out on October 14, a downpour began and continued unabated for five days and nights. Even when it let up, heavy rains fell during the afternoon and night.

Profiting from the experience of Mendendorp Force, the battalion had left behind its gas masks, helmets, and mess kits. The first day of the march, as the climb got steeper, the men began to discard raincoats, shelter halves, and blankets; thereafter, most of them had no protection from the chilling nightly rains. The mud on the track was so deep that they sank into it up to their knees; some of them had to be pulled out. The mountain streams they had to cross became raging torrents, with currents strong enough to sweep a man downstream.

Soon the troops were not only wet and cold but hungry. They had a few C-rations but depended mostly on the Australian ration of rice, corned beef, and tea. It was so hard to get a fire going that they often ate the food cold and threw away the tea; nor could they sterilize their eating utensils. Some of the corned beef was contaminated. Diarrhea and dysentery affected almost everybody, many of the men so severely that they had to cut away the seat of their trousers. Falling down beside the track so sick and weak that 'they were ready to call it "quits" and die', they were picked up and cared for by the medical officers bringing up the rear. Many felt they owed their lives to these doctors.

In the words of the top sergeant of Company E,

It was one green hell to Jaure. We were up and down continuously; the company would be stretched over two or three miles. We'd start at six every morning by cooking rice or trying to. Two guys would work together. If they could start a fire which was hard because the wood was wet even when you cut deep into the center of the log, they'd mix a little bully beef into a canteen cup with rice, to get the starchy taste out of it. Sometimes we'd take turns blowing on sparks trying to start a fire, and keep it up for two hours without success . . . The men got weaker; guys began to lag back . . . An officer stayed at the end of the line to keep driving the stragglers. There wasn't any way of evacuating to the rear. Men with sprained ankles hobbled along as well as they could, driven on by fear of being left behind.

At Ghost Mountain 'it was cold . . . if we stopped we froze. If we moved we sweated.' When the going got steeper, the haggard men, weak, filthy, and mud-caked, could barely pick themselves up at the start of a day's march. *Our strength is about gone,* the sergeant wrote in his diary. *We seem to climb straight up for hours, then down again. God, will it never end?* It took them seven hours to crawl the last 2,000 feet of the 9,000-foot divide.

Jaure was reached on October 28. The same day, the battalion began moving out on the track toward Buna (Mendendorp Force was already patrolling the track toward Wairopi), down the eastern slope of the Owen Stanley Range. Its destination was Bofu, where it was to turn left on the flanking movement to support the Australians. En route to Bofu, it stopped at Natunga, a village in the foothills where an airdropping ground was made ready. While rations, helmets, boots, and other supplies were dropped from transport planes, the troops of the 2d Battalion had more than a week of rest. But this was not enough to repair the damage inflicted on them by the climb over the Kapa Kapa Track – one of the most punishing ordeals of World War II. The battalion had nearly been destroyed as a fighting unit.

Worst of all was the dawning realization that the ordeal had been undergone to no purpose. The climb over the Kapa Kapa Track had been unnecessary. Almost as soon as the 2d Battalion started up the track, reports came to 32d Division headquarters that there were level fields of kunai grass near the coast – like that at Wanigela – where troops could be landed by air. Several were quickly prepared. The remaining battalions of the 126th Regiment, as well as the entire 128th Regiment, were flown over the Owen Stanleys.

The fiasco of the Kapa Kapa Track had stemmed from impatience and ignorance. The report of the reconnaissance party that the track was practicable for marching was probably inspired by the urge – common in all armies – to tell generals what they wanted to hear. In turn, the generals had believed it because they wanted to believe it.

The most promising place for an airfield on the coast was at Pangani, a native village about 30 miles south of Buna, in the area where the northern coast of Cape Nelson juts out into the Solomon Sea. From this point the 126th Regiment could turn west to join with the Australians, and the 128th Regiment could march north, when the time came, on Buna.

The 128th Regiment then in camp near Port Moresby, was to form the bulk of MacArthur's coastal force, eventually called Warren Force. The officer appointed to command it was Brigadier General Hanford MacNider, a member of MacArthur's own staff. MacNider was a personage; an imposing Iowan of fifty-three with a fine record in World War I, he had been, after the war, national commander of the American Legion, Assistant Secretary of War, and U.S. Minister to Canada.

MacNider's force could be flown to Wanigela, near the southern coast of Cape Nelson, and march across the neck of the cape to Pongani; but how was it to be supplied with rations and ammunition? Airdropping could not be depended upon entirely, because the available planes were strained to support the men on the Kokoda Track.

The alternative was supply by sea. It was hazardous. The coast between Milne Bay and Buna is washed by waters foul with coral reefs, shunned by all the navies of the world. The native villages along the coast have no jetties. These problems were later solved in the Southwest Pacific by landing craft, but MacArthur had none.

The solution was to use a fleet of small ships – trawlers or luggers – rounded up from island traders and fishermen. Still reeking of copra or fish, the trawlers had sails to be used when their asthmatic engines broke down, and dirty awnings spread aft over sun-scorched decks. The crews, recruited by Mac-

Arthur's Small Ships Section, were Filipinos, Malayans, or New Guinea natives; the masters were middle-aged Australian civilians. On each trawler the U.S. Army installed two machine guns on shoulder-high mounts ahead of the wheelhouse and furnished soldiers to operate them; and at each mast flapped a brand-new American flag.

These shabby little warships gave point to an exclamation by an American general on the scene: 'Goddam war's gone all old-fashioned on us here!'

The first trawler to chug away from the Port Moresby wharf on October 12 was the *King John*, which carried the commander of the fleet, Lieutenant Colonel Laurence A. McKenny. He was the 32d Division's Quartermaster, a cheerful, affable gentleman who before the war had been the principal of a high school in Detroit. Following closely behind the flagship was the *Timoshenko*.

By nightfall both ships were well out into the Coral Sea and two days later were entering Milne Bay, where they were to take on supplies and pick up the local representative of the Small Ships Section, Lieutenant Adam Bruce Fahnestock.

Tying up for the night at Gili Gili wharf under clouds of mosquitoes, the passengers saw Milne Bay being transformed into a great military base, with coconut-log roads, thatched roof warehouses, and docks for the freighters that stood out in the harbor. Along the shore were evidences of the enemy attack: Japanese tanks mired in the mud, Japanese barges rocking in the waves that rippled through the swamps, and the Australian freighter *Anshun* on its side near the wharf. Next morning the supplies were loaded and Lieutenant Fahnestock came aboard the *King John*. A personable man in his early thirties, he was the Bruce Fahnestock whose South Seas voyages with his brother Sheridan, just before the war, had been well publicized.

Leaving Milne Bay, the two trawlers chugged cautiously along the upper coast, following a channel recently marked by the Australians, and arrived off Wanigela shortly after noon on October 16.

Colonel McKenny expected to unload his supplies at Wanigela and return to Milne Bay; but when he went ashore in the dinghy and located General MacNider, he received a shock. MacNider told him that two battalions of the 128th Infantry were then marching across the neck of Cape Nelson to Pongani.

Therefore the trawlers were to sail around Cape Nelson and land at Pongani. Moreover, they were to carry forward a company of the 128th that had just come in by air from Port Moresby.

The following afternoon, without waiting for the rest of the fleet (plagued by the troubles that beset such ships, the remaining six did not arrive for several days), the colonel was ready to sail. Fifty-six men were rowed out to the *King John*, forty-six to the *Timoshenko*. Along with the soldiers climbing aboard the *King John* came Barney Darnton of the New York *Times*, elated at having been given permission to go forward with the troops.

Hoisting anchors, the two trawlers snaked along the uncharted waters off Cape Nelson all afternoon and most of the night. At the prow of each crouched a native boy who during the day signaled to the helmsman with a flick of his hand when green reef water came into view, and when darkness fell probed for reefs with a plumbline. The men on the packed decks watched the phosphorescent waters below and the great wheeling constellations above.

Nobody slept much that night. Aboard the *King John*, Fahnestock stood on deck directing the navigation, while in the cabin below by the flickering light of a swinging kerosene lantern McKenny and the combat officers studied enlargements of an aerial map of Pongani and planned the landing. Darnton made notes for his story, his greatest story – two little fishing trawlers carrying General MacArthur's first amphibious operation against the Japanese!

By three o'clock next morning, October 18, the trawlers had safely rounded Cape Nelson. They hove to, engines stopped, waiting for dawn. At the first yellow light in the sky they proceeded at half-speed until the palm-fringed shore came into view and they could recognize the huts that were Pongani. Dropping anchor about a quarter of a mile offshore, the *King John* and *Timoshenko* got ready to launch their landing parties. It was 7.55. The morning trade wind flung out the American flags at the mastheads.

Suddenly a bomber appeared, circling overhead, a twin-tailed two-motored bomber, unidentified. The question in everybody's mind was written by Darnton in his notebook: *Ours, or theirs?*

Two bombs came down but missed. At the first bomb the machine gunners on both trawlers opened up. The bomber veered off to the southeast but soon returned, firing its own machine gun, and dropped two bombs that exploded on the port side and stern of the *King John*. Then the bomber flew off in the direction of Cape Nelson. It was later determined to be an American B-25 that had not expected to find friendly ships in those waters.

Eighteen men on the *King John* had been wounded, two fatally, several seriously. Barney Darnton, struck in the head by a bomb fragment, died in the rowboat as he was being carried ashore. Bruce Fahnestock, hit in the spine, lived only five minutes after reaching shore. That evening, after the rations and ammunition had been landed, the *King John* and *Timoshenko* started back to Wanigela with the wounded and the dead.

Colonel McKenny, who had received a bomb splinter in his hand, went on with his job of setting up the dumps at Pongani. Next morning his depleted landing party on the strange and possibly hostile shore had a visitor, an Australian officer who reported that there were no Japanese either in the Pongani area or at the next village three miles up the coast, Mendaropu, near which were some usable huts at an abandoned settlement called Emo Mission. McKenny moved his command post to Mendaropu, where coconut palms leaned over thatched huts built on stilts.

Several days later the rest of the trawlers came up, bringing more troops, the men of the two battalions who had been sent up the inland track from Wanigela. They had found it under water from the flooding of a river and been unable to proceed. When the six trawlers anchored offshore at Mendaropu, outriggers went through the breakers to unload them, looking like props in a South Seas travelogue. On October 21 they brought in the regimental commander, Colonel J. Tracy Hale, Jr, and a few days later General MacNider and his staff.

But MacNider's coastal force was not to move forward for several weeks. General MacArthur, watching events at Guadalcanal, where the Japanese were sending in strong reinforcements, had to consider the possibility that the enemy would be victorious in the Solomons and would then be able to turn his full strength on New Guinea. MacArthur had even prepared, in that event, plans for a withdrawal from the northern coast and even from New Guinea.

In any case, MacArthur's preparations for hemming the Japanese on the Buna beachhead were falling behind schedule. Much depended on the Australians who were advancing over the mountains toward Kokoda; and in his opinion, as he informed General Blamey on October 21, their progress over the Kokoda Track was 'NOT, repeat NOT, satisfactory'.

CHAPTER VII

HORII'S FIGHTING WITHDRAWAL

When General MacArthur fired off his peremptory message to
General Blamey on October 21, the Australians on the Kokoda
Track, slowed down by driving gusty rains, had just come up
against the jungle fortress prepared by General Horii's Stanley
Shitai at the deep ravine beyond Myola.

The battle for Eora Creek was just beginning, and it was to
last for seven days. By October 21, General Horii had brought
up reinforcements from Kokoda and Buna and ordered his
forces to hold at Eora until October 28. He needed time to prepare his next – and last – line of defense. This was not to be at
Kokoda, as the Australians expected, but at Oivi, on the road
from Kokoda to Buna, the spur in the foothills where in late
July the Japanese had routed the 39th Battalion. Command at
Oivi was given to competent Colonel Yazawa, and his orders
were to construct fortifications strong enough to 'hold out for a
long period against a numerically stronger enemy'. He was, in
effect, to buy time for reinforcements to be landed at Buna
from Rabaul.

The Australians moving down through the cold, rain-
dripping jungle into the gloomy gorge of Eora Creek on
October 20 were men of Brigadier Lloyd's 16th Brigade, which
had just taken over from Eather's weary 25th Brigade. Lloyd's
men, still fresh, in 'fine fettle' and as yet unaffected by malaria,
routed the Japanese outposts in the ravine. But next morning
when they attempted to ascend the ridge above the ravine, they
were stopped by withering fire from above and had to dig in.

They had come up against Horii's strong fortifications – a central keep about 300 yards across, from which radiated machine-gun pits, some strengthened with logs and many roofed for concealment. From this position the Japanese could not be dislodged. They had only to fire into the treetops below to kill or maim their attackers, sheltering there in two-man weapon pits. General Horii himself inspected his 'forest fort' on October 25, an occasion marked by the issue of a cup of sake to all officers. *How tasteful it was*, one of them wrote in his diary.

The battle dragged on, much of it at close quarters. The Australians clinging like leeches to the sharp slope, often in a cold, driving rain, could not move by day from their pits, or even light twigs to make hot tea, without drawing fire. Their only food was the dehydrated emergency ration, eaten dry and cold; their only water was the little they could catch in their rubber capes or suck from the roots of the 'water tree'.

By October 27, alarm at Allied Force Headquarters had mounted to such a pitch that General Allen, at Myola, was relieved of command of 7th Division and replaced by General 'Bloody George' Vasey.

On the following morning, October 28, as General Vasey was arriving at Myola to take over command, the Japanese on their heights above Eora Creek increased their harassment, bowling down grenades on the men clinging to the slopes below and all day directing heavy fire whenever the Australians tried to attack. Not until nightfall did the fire let up.

This effort effectively covered Horii's withdrawal. When the Australians in the gathering darkness smashed through the outposts and into the central positions, the Japanese rear guard ran screaming into the jungle.

The Australians lost no time in taking up the pursuit. Reaching Alola on October 30, they found that the Japanese had just pulled out, so recently that their cooking pots were still warm. At Alola, strewn with remnants of the stores abandoned months before and overrun by rats, the pursuers were split into two forces. General Vasey ordered Eather's 25th Brigade north to take Kokoda and turned Lloyd's 16th Brigade eastward on a secondary track to capture Oivi.

For Lloyd's men November 1 was 'a happy sort of day'. Most of them had had a hot meal the night before, for the first time in days. As they moved out, the only danger they encountered was 'dive-bombing' from U.S. planes that were trying to drop picks and shovels on the Alola dropping ground. At native villages they found green bananas and papaws – the first fruit they had had since leaving Port Moresby. Next day the track began to descend, and before long they came out into flat ground and sunshine. Their spirits rose in the realization that they had left behind 'the pouring, dripping, misty ranges'. With the good feel of the sun on their backs, with their hunger assuaged by the marrow, yams, and taro they found in native gardens, they were happy. The native carriers stuck yellow flowers in their hair, 'adding almost an air of festivity to the march'.

On November 2, Eather's men entered Kokoda and found that the Japanese had been gone for two days. Next morning airdropping began and engineers began preparing the airstrip for landings; in the afternoon General Vasey arrived and raised the Australian flag. It was a time of great rejoicing for the natives, bedecked with garlands of flowers. Their drums carried the good news across the hills.

In the midst of this rejoicing, General Vasey received some troubling news: pilots flying over the coastal area reported seeing two destroyers and two transports off Buna. He ordered Lloyd to move forward toward Oivi at full strength immediately.

The officer carrying Vasey's order found Lloyd at the place where the secondary track entered the muddy, corduroyed 'Kokoda Road' leading from Kokoda to Buna. The two officers, impatient to begin the advance, had just begun walking down the road, ahead of the troops, when Japanese fire erupted from the jungle. This was the first of a series of rear guard actions; but Lloyd did not let them hold him up, and by the morning of November 5 was mounting a strong attack on Oivi with two battalions.

His third battalion was probing, at General Vasey's suggestion, a track to the south of Oivi, paralleling the Kokoda Road and connected with it by several north–south tracks that might be used in a flanking movement. One of these led to Gorari, three miles east of Oivi.

Gorari was to be the key point in the battle for Oivi.

On the first day of the battle, Lloyd's two battalions on the Kokoda Road could make no progress. They had come up against the position strongly fortified by Colonel Yazawa. From the high ground where Oivi stood – a few native huts set in a grove of young rubber trees – a number of thickly wooded spurs thrust westward toward the attackers, and from these spurs the Japanese poured down deadly fire from guns emplaced in thick bunkers.

Colonel Yazawa was determined to hold out at least long enough for General Horii and the main body of the Japanese forces to cross the Kumusi River. Horii was then some ten miles east of Oivi near Wairopi, where his men were resting and preparing for the crossing.

When General Vasey learned on November 6 that Lloyd had been stopped at Oivi and was suffering heavy casualties, he sent Eather and his 25th Brigade down the parallel tracks to take the Japanese from the rear at Gorari.

Horii had anticipated this movement. Several days before, he had sent a battalion westward from Wairopi to defend Gorari. From well dug-in positions they threw back Eather's attack on November 9 and even erupted in fierce counterattacks, at heavy cost to the Australians. But Eather's men persisted, and though the fighting surged back and forth all day on November 10, at dusk in a sweeping attack they captured Gorari.

The fall of Gorari upset the Japanese timetable. Oivi had now become untenable and Colonel Yazawa began his withdrawal at once. Unable to use the road through Gorari, and faced with the responsibility of evacuating not only some nine hundred men but his general, for General Horii was then at Oivi on an inspection trip, Yazawa led his forces in a stealthy night withdrawal off the Kokoda Road into the jungle on a little-known track leading northeast to the Kumusi River at a point north of Wairopi. From there his men were to plod through the sago swamps along the left bank of the river, their objective the mouth of the Kumusi, 12 miles north of Gona.

The time involved in this march was too much for General Horii, who was impatient to rejoin his forces on the coast. When the marchers came to a place where, on the far bank of the Kumusi, a track led due east to Gona, he decided to cross the river.

On a log raft the general and four men of his headquarters party pushed out into the swift current, which seemed to the Japanese 'unbelievably rapid', compared to the rivers in Japan.

The raft overturned. Soldiers jumped into the river to try to save their general, but were soon themselves in trouble in the rushing waters. General Horii and Colonel Tanaka fended them off, saying, 'Don't bother about us older men. Save yourselves. You are young and strong.' These were their last words before they were swept away, and never seen again.

On the Kokoda Road east of Gorari, rear guards successfully covered the retreat of the main Japanese force, about 1,200 strong. They began crossing the Kumusi at Wairopi after dark on November 12, guided by a bonfire built by their engineers. They had no bridge. The wooden bridge built by the Japanese after the Australians destroyed the wire-rope bridge had been destroyed by incendiary bombs dropped from Allied planes, rebuilt, and then destroyed again and again, so that after a time the Japanese engineers had not troubled to replace it, but simply brought forward supplies from the coast in a basket that ran by pulley on a wire. Even this wire was not immune to attack. Low-flying American aircraft managed to cut it with machine gun fire, a feat that seemed 'wonderful' to the Japanese. 'A circus in the air!' exclaimed a young Japanese engineer. And war correspondent Seizo Okada noted that the engineer 'spoke in pure admiration of the daring and skillful performance of the enemy fliers, without a shade of hostility in his tone. There was no longer the least suspicion of hostile feeling or fighting spirit in any unit or soldier. The only thing that occupied our minds was to get back to the coast as soon as possible.'

After standing in line in the darkness for hours. Okada boarded one of the six-man folding boats that were ferrying the troops across the rushing Kumusi. When he reached the far bank he pushed on through the night as fast as he could to get away from the enemy planes that were expected by daylight. Next day in a coffee plantation about seven miles from the coast, he found shelter in a native hut.

Along the road that passed by this hut, lines of Japanese soldiers who had crossed the Kumusi moved day and night toward the coast. They had long, shaggy hair and beards. 'Their uniforms were soiled with blood and mud and sweat, and torn to pieces. There were infantrymen without rifles, men walking on bare feet, men wearing blankets or straw rice bags instead of uniforms, men reduced to skin and bones plodding along with the help of a stick, men gasping and crawling on the ground.' All carried what remained of their rice and taros either tied in a corner of a blanket or swinging from a belt or slung over a shoulder. Once in a while a sturdy young fellow marched by with a quick step, but many of the soldiers fell exhausted on the side of the road, 'some of them lying there for a while and struggling to their feet again, while others stirred no more.'

Okada, walking to the coast in the hope of being taken back to Rabaul on one of the transports that were expected any day to bring reinforcements, passed by a hospital where so many sick and wounded were laid on straw mats in the jungle that there was hardly room to walk between them. The men brought from the mountains had eaten anything – leaves, grass, even dirt – so that many could no longer digest food and were dying of starvation. Others, tossing about and groaning in delirium, were victims of malaria.

Some had gone mad. One day while Okada was sitting on the beach, gazing at the wide expanse of calm, empty sea, he was joined by an emaciated young captain who began to talk wildly about the ship that was coming to take him back to his wife and children in Japan, about such delicacies as *o-sushi* (vinegared rice and fish) and about the gold that was to be found along the coast. 'New Guinea has been famous for its gold mines, as I suppose you know. Did you ever see Charlie Chaplin in *The Gold Rush*? A damned funny picture, wasn't it?' He was still rattling on, his eyes fixed on the distant horizon, when a hospital attendant appeared, took his hand as if he had been a child, and led him away.

Late that afternoon Okada saw a smudge of smoke on the horizon. The ships had come. That evening, in a tropical downpour, barges carried Okada, along with the sick, wounded, and prisoners of war, out to the anchorage where they were to go aboard the transports for the return to Rabaul as soon as the ships were unloaded. In one of the barges waiting in the calm gray sea flattened by the rain was Father Benson, the priest of Gona. Looking up at one of the huge warships, Benson saw hundreds of men swarming down the rope ladders, followed by bags of rice and casks and cases of provisions heaved down from the decks above.

It was the evening of November 17. The six warships landed

a formidable force of about a thousand men. Along with three hundred replacements for the 144th Infantry and the regiment's new commander, Colonel Hiroshi Yamamoto, there arrived the 3d Battalion, 229th Infantry, an excellent combat unit with experience in China, Hong Kong, and Java. The newcomers were sent to the Buna area, where Yamamoto took over command from Captain Yoshitatsu Yasuda of the Japanese Navy. This was the area where the U.S. 32d Division was to attack from its coastal positions.

Gona and Sanananda, where the Australians were to attack, were also reinforced. Colonel Yokoyama, who after the death of General Horii took charge of all Japanese forces at Gona and Sanananda, sent to Gona about eight hundred troops, including some highly valued jungle fighters from Formosa. At Sanananda and on the road leading to it he placed the bulk of his combat effectives together with some engineers and naval construction troops and two mountain gun batteries.

Along the 11-mile front leading from Gona to Cape Endaiadere beyond Buna, the Japanese, beginning in September, had constructed hundreds of coconut-log bunkers reinforced with steel plates and rails and oil drums filled with sand. They were seven or eight feet above ground because the water table ruled out trenches or dugout, but they were so skillfully concealed with earth, rocks, palm branches, and quick-growing vegetation that they merged with their surroundings.

Unaware of these formidable well-hidden positions, the Australians and Americans moved out confidently into the attack.

CHAPTER VIII

THE ALLIES' OFFENSIVE BEGINS—
AND STALLS

On the day the Australian flag was raised over Kokoda, November 2, General MacArthur named November 15 as the tentative date for the combined Australian-American attack against the Japanese enclave on the coast.

The general flew to Port Moresby on November 6 (leaving his wife and child behind in Brisbane) and moved into Government House, which for more than half a century had been the residence of the Australian governors. An airy, one-story building shaded by coconut palms, set on a sloping grassy hill about a mile north of the port area, it had been refurbished in preparation for MacArthur's arrival. Its wide veranda, commanding a fine view of the blue-green harbor and brown hills beyond, had been screened and furnished with wicker chairs. Bedrooms had been refurnished, bathrooms equipped with modern plumbing, and the staff of nine native houseboys had been uniformed in fresh white sarongs, or lap-laps, bordered in red with a blue star in the corner.

The order for the offensive was eagerly awaited by the troops of the U.S. 32d Division, who for several weeks had been encamped in great discomfort on the broiling New Guinea coast around Pongani. Under their helmets or cloth fisherman's hats their faces were bearded and dirty. They were hungry; the little trawlers had not been able to bring in adequate rations. Their uniforms and shoes were beginning to wear out. On their skin jungle ulcers had erupted, because the green dye applied to their fatigues stopped up the cloth so that no air could get through; and many were already affected by dysentery and malaria: their name for Pognani was 'Fever Ridge'. All in all, they were impatient to get the campaign over with and return to civilization and they saw no reason why it could not be done in a matter of days. Their officers were convinced that Buna, only 30 miles away, 'could be had by walking in and taking over.'

But when the order for the offensive finally came on November 3, it contained a shocker. It stipulated that the Americans on the coast were not to move forward until further notice. At this, 'the lid really blew off'. The official reason for the stipulation, that time was needed to bring up supplies and that it was dangerous for the Americans to go into action before the Australians (who were just then advancing on Oivi) could move up and cover their left flank, was simply not believed.

'Opinions were freely expressed by officers of all ranks,' a War Department observer on the scene reported, 'that the only reason for the order was a political one. G.H.Q. was afraid to turn the Americans loose and let them capture Buna because it would be a blow to the prestige of the Australians who had fought the long hard battle all through the Owen Stanley Mountains, and who therefore should be the ones to capture Buna.'

Thus was surfaced the suspicion, and even distrust of Allies, inherent in coalition warfare.

At this point a powerful voice was raised in Port Moresby in favor of turning the Americans loose. General Kenney, while considering it only natural that General Blamey 'wanted to see his Australians get in on the kill' rather than 'watching the Americans rush in and reap the glory,' tried to convince General MacArthur that General Hardin's 32d Division should be allowed to jump off on November 10 before the rainy season, expected in mid-November, set in. But MacArthur, after a conference with Blamey, decided that Harding was to wait until General Vasey's Australians had crossed the Kumusi and were well advanced into the coastal plain.

Hot in pursuit of the Japanese, Vasey's troops pressed along the road to the Kumusi on the morning of November 12, but were held up by the enemy's determined rear guard and did not reach the Kumusi until the following afternoon. There they learned from natives that the Japanese had crossed the night before. The Australians' crossing had to await the air-dropping, next day, of steel cable and tools. The cable, carried to the far bank by swimmers, was rigged with bos'n's chairs (which the Australians called 'flying foxes') and by nightfall a small suspension bridge was ready. Darkness and heavy rain then caused postponement, but on the following day, November 15, the balky flying foxes and sagging suspension bridge enabled the 25th Brigade to reach the far bank of the Kumusi.

That afternoon the 16th Brigade arrived at the Kumusi in high spirits, having had two days' rest. The men were accompanied by a horse the Japanese had left behind, his back loaded with their supplies. At the river bank they found the scene 'reminiscent of an old English fair or Irish market day.' Interspersed among the troops in mud-stained green uniforms waiting their turn to cross were native carriers in bright-colored lap-laps, with flowers in their hair and sprigs of shrubs in their leather bracelets. The hazardous suspension bridge and flying foxes were tackled next day 'in something of a carnival spirit.'

In much the same spirit, the Americans on the coast were at last preparing to move against the Japanese at Buna. Their timetable had been moved up, and for this they could thank events at Guadalcanal, where beginning on November 12 a fierce naval battle was being fought. General Blamey, fearful that the Japanese might be successful at Guadalcanal and then be in a position to land massive reinforcements in New Guinea, felt that the Allies should forestall them at once.

Doughty little General Harding was elated, for he had felt all along that Buna might be 'easy pickings', defended only by 'a shell of sacrifice troops.'

His target was a three-mile-long strip of coast stretching from Buna Village, on the left, to Cape Endaiadere, a promontory on the right.

On the left, the approach to the target was by an inland trail that forked as it neared the coast, one fork leading to Buna Village, the other to Buna Government Station (usually and mistakenly referred to in afteraction reports as 'Buna Mission'), a mile to the east of the village and separated from it by a wide estuary, Entrance Creek. The area between the forks was called the Triangle. There the attack was to be made by Harding's 126th Regiment as soon as it had completed its movement to the coast.

On the right, Cape Endaiadere was to be taken by his 128th Regiment, split to advance on two approaches. One was by a coastal trail, the other by an inland trail that ran between two airstrips – Old Strip (the original Buna Station strip) and New Strip, built by the Japanese. The 128th's 1st Battalion was to march up the beach. Its 3d Battalion was to march a short distance inland, as far as Dobodura, where General Kenney was building an airfield, then turn north to attack along the trail between the two airstrips. Its 2d Battalion, in reserve, was to follow the 3d as far as Dobodura and remain there to help get the airfield ready.

The move forward began gaily in an atmosphere that one officer remembered as 'like the eve of a celebration to come. We were to go in and "raise the flag" and there was to be a great victory for the American forces with very little effort on our part.' Natives said the enemy was withdrawing his outposts; Intelligence estimated that Buna was garrisoned by not more than a battalion; Air maintained that there was

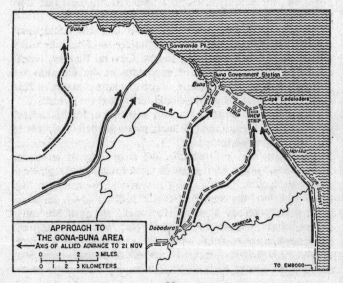

APPROACH TO
THE GONA-BUNA AREA
◀── AXIS OF ALLIED ADVANCE TO 21 NOV

'nothing around Buna but a few sick Japs.'

Before nightfall on November 14 the beach force was well up the coast at Embogo, where the Quartermaster, Colonel McKenny, had set up ration and ammunition dumps; and the inland force was on its way to Dobodura.

The men of both battalions carried nothing heavier than light machine guns. Their 81-mm. mortars and 50-caliber machine guns, as well as ammunition, rations, and other supplies for the whole force were to be brought up the coast in trawlers on the afternoon of November 16 and landed at Hariko, about 13 miles north of Embogo – and less than 5 miles from the Japanese outposts at Cape Endaiadere.

Just to make victory doubly certain, Harding and his artillery officer, Brigadier General Albert W. Waldron, had been trying to get some tanks and heavy artillery to use in the attack on Buna. They received little support from General MacArthur, and for this the responsibility partly lay with General Kenney, who argued that tanks and artillery had no place in jungle warfare. Kenney's influence over MacArthur remained very strong – strangely so in a matter concerning ground action in the jungle, on which he could have had no real knowledge. Loyal to Air, Kenney maintained that 'The artillery in this theater flies.'

The American officers on the Buna coast disagreed; and turned for help to the Australians. Lend-lease light tanks were then at Milne Bay, but could not be brought forward. With the artillery, they had better luck. One of the flat-bottomed, motor-driven barges the Japanese had left behind at Milne Bay could be used to transport the guns. Shuttling back and forth, the barge brought up four 25-pounder guns and two 3.7-inch mountain howitzers, also their Australian crews.

In a daring commando landing ahead of the troops, General Waldron took the two mountain howitzers to the front in the Japanese barge on the evening of November 15. Moving cautiously up the coast in the blackness, about midnight the barge grounded at Cape Sudest, a headland about halfway between Embogo and Hariko. There was no sign of life, only the sound of breakers and lashing palm fronds. Putting the howitzers and crews ashore before daybreak, Waldron returned in the empty barge to pick up two of the 25-pounder guns. His ammunition was to be brought up next day in General Mac-

Nider's command ship, the trawler *Kelton*.

The morning of November 16 dawned fine and clear. The troops at Embogo, after a breakfast of coffee and 'cracker mush' (hard Australian crackers softened with a mixture of water and dried milk), started up the beach trail toward Cape Sudest, where they had been ordered to halt and await the arrival of the *Kelton* with General MacNider and Colonel Hale, the 128th Infantry's commander.

Touching at Embogo that morning, MacNider took aboard the *Kelton* some war correspondents and newsreel cameramen who were clamoring for rides to the front, eager to be on the scene of General MacArthur's first victory over the Japanese.

The optimism was contagious. When the *Kelton* reached Cape Sudest, where the troops were waiting, MacNider ordered the trawler not to stop, but to continue up the coast, this in spite of a warning from an officer on the beach, who ran out into the surf and waved his shirt to the rear to indicate that there were no friendly troops ahead. MacNider also, according to Colonel Hale, ignored Hale's protest against a landing on an unprotected coast almost in sight of the enemy. This episode contributed to the acrimony that had already developed between the two men.

Around noon MacNider and his party went ashore at Hariko and before long were joined by troops quickly ordered forward to protect him. Hastening the unloading of the ammunition from the *Kelton*, MacNider sent the trawler back to Embogo to pick up a Quartermaster officer.

Early in the afternoon came the first indication that the battle for Buna might be costly. The men at Hariko saw American bombers over the Buna area being attacked by a heavy volume of antiaircraft fire; one bomber went down in flames. A reconnaissance patrol ran into Japanese machine-gun fire from Cape Endaiadere. Artillery support was called for, and the mountain howitzers were brought up. At 4.40 the crews fired on Cape Endaiadere.

At the time the howitzers fired, the supply ships were just beginning to leave Embogo, with more than an hour's sail before they could reach Hariko. They had no air cover, because Allied planes had to leave the coast at five o'clock in order to cross the Owen Stanley Mountains before dark. But for more than a month the sky had been free of enemy planes. Nobody was worried.

In the lead was the largest ship in the supply convoy, the schooner *Alacrity*, towing a small steel barge. She carried most of the ammunition for the task force and had aboard, among other passengers, the Ordnance officer, young First Lieutenant John E. Harbert, also about forty native ammunition carriers, and a twenty-nine-man portable hospital – a new type of medical unit with its equipment packed in small boxes. Next was the trawler *Minniemura* taking General Harding to the front, along with his aides, an observer from the United States, and an Australian war correspondent, Geoffrey Reading. Last was General Waldron's Japanese barge, loaded with two 25-pounder guns and crews.

A number of newspapermen and cameramen had to be left behind for lack of space. One of the most disappointed was Tom Fisher, an Australian cameraman, who since October had been photographing the American advance up the coast. But Fisher was to be given another chance. Soon after the departure of the supply convoy, the *Kelton* returned with MacNider's request for a Quartermaster officer. This created a problem, for the *Kelton* could not be spared. It was solved when an unidentified trawler was seen making her way up the coast. She was hailed, and Colonel McKenny went aboard, taking along Fisher and another Australian photographer, Frank Bagnall. They found that the trawler was the *Bonwin*, loaded with ammunition and oil drums, her only passengers some native carriers.

Aboard the *Minnemura*, Geoffrey Reading thought, This is the way to travel!

He had flown to the coast that morning to cover the American advance on Buna. Having just spent two weeks on the Kokoda Track, he had been disturbed by the insouciance of the Americans as they embarked on the perilous advance by sea. While he was being rowed out to the *Minnemura* by young Captain John R. Keegan, the black fin of a shark cleaved the water and circled them. Keegan only laughed and threatened to capsize the dinghy. A worse shock was in store for Reading when he studied the map in the *Minnemura*'s wheelhouse. It showed that Hariko was in full view of Cape

Endaiadere; enemy spotters must have seen MacNider's landing. He asked Keegan, 'Do you see anything funny in that?' But the reply, 'Boy, that sure is solemn,' was so nonchalant that Reading's uneasiness vanished.

He felt pleasantly relaxed as he sat on the forward hatch in the afternoon sunshine, watching the prow slicing through waves in whose troughs flying fish were scudding. At the bow stood a native boy with a red flower in his hair, throwing out a plumb line and calling the depths. The voyage was soon over. At twenty minutes to seven, as the sun was sinking behind the shoreline, the *Minnemura* was rounding Cape Sudest and her passengers could see the *Alacrity* ahead, dropping anchor off Hariko.

Reading was chatting with some soldiers and General Harding was going aft to have supper when the faint sound of airplane motors was heard to starboard far out at sea. Then black dots began to appear in the sky. Reading counted seventeen. Everybody stopped talking and the silence itself was the interrogation: 'Our, or theirs?' As the planes came nearer Reading saw their blunt noses and said, 'I think they are Zeros.' The Australian skipper took a long look through his binoculars and swung the wheel hard toward shore. Captain Keegan picked up an ammunition belt and fed it to the port gun. The native at the prow slipped over the side and began to swim for shore.

The Japanese planes passed quickly over the trawler and disappeared; but ten minutes later they reappeared, this time coming up very fast from the south. Three swooped down, first on the *Bonwin,* less than a mile behind the *Minnemura,* and then on General Waldron's slow Japanese barge bringing up the rear.

On the *Bonwin,* as soon as the planes were identified as enemy Colonel McKenny ordered everyone to go either into the main cabin aft or a small cabin forward and lie flat. McKenny, Tom Fisher, and several others went into the main cabin. Frank Bagnall and two natives went into the forward cabin. While the men were lying on the decks or the cabins, the Zeros swooped down firing. Bullets passed just above the men lying prone.

In the respite that followed, Bagnall realized that the planes were climbing to make another run. He ran up on deck, dived over the side and swam away from the ship. Looking back he saw that incendiary bullets had set the gasoline drums on the deck afire and that burning gasoline was pouring into the main cabin. There was no escape for Colonel McKenny, Tom Fisher, and others trapped inside. Before Bagnall's eyes the *Bonwin* was enveloped in flames and sank. Some distance away, her dinghy was drifting, cut loose by gunfire. Bagnall climbed into it, plugged bullet holes with pieces of his clothing, and, using a piece of board for a paddle, picked up five survivors and started for shore.

On the Japanese barge, when the men saw fourteen planes high overhead, one of the Australian gunners shouted 'Good old Yanks!' But they soon realized that the planes were the top cover for three Zeros that were already diving on the barge. Each Zero made three runs, firing tracer bullets that ripped into gasoline drums. Soon the barge was afire in swirling clouds of black smoke. Five Australians and one American were killed and sixteen men were wounded. Lacking a lifeboat, the survivors took to the water, General Waldron among them.

The *Minnemura* was next. After the disappearance of her native lookout, she stuck fast on a reef and was thus a sitting duck for the Zeros. Four dived over once with silent guns, swept by, banked steeply, and then raced at the ship firing tracer bullets and cannon shells. General Harding, crouching behind some ration boxes in the stern, fired with his rifle at the pilots of the Zeros, who were not much more than seventy-five feet above him; but his fire had no effect. Neither did that of the machine guns: on the port side Keegan's gun jammed and he was hit in the leg; on the starboard side the machine gunner got off only a few rounds before he fell to the deck mortally wounded. Some of the wounded were loaded in the ship's dinghy and propelled to the shore by swimmers. After the dinghy was on its way, General Harding dived overboard.

The Japanese continued to strafe and bomb the *Minnemura* and the men making for the shore. Geoffrey Reading, diving out as far as he could, so deep that his hands and knees touched coral, heard cries and groans when he surfaced, felt a violent shock when two bombs came down on either side of the ship, and saw a Zero making two passes at the dinghy.

Up ahead the *Alacrity* was a bonfire. The first strafing runs started fires more dangerous than those on the other ships because of her heavy load of ammunition. After her machine guns had been put out of action, the survivors of the hospital unit – four members had been killed and five wounded – got off a few rounds with submachine guns and rifles, but their commander, fearing an explosion, ordered them overboard. The forty natives had already jumped over the side, but before they had had time to disperse, a bomb fell among then, killing all but a dozen.

Lieutenant Harbert was standing in the *Alacrity*'s towed steel barge taking on ammunition for delivery to the shore. When the attack began, the men helping him took cover, but when they saw that he remained upright, throwing overboard the flaming debris that fell on the barge, they went back to work. Taking aboard some wounded men and two medical chests, Harbert led a party that pulled the barge to the shore. His bravery that afternoon won him the Distinguished Service Cross.

The tropical night fell suddenly and as suddenly all the Japanese planes were gone. By that time the fires had reached the ammunition on the ships: rockets and flares went up like fireworks and the sky was alight for miles. In the red glare on the water rescue expeditions sent out from the shore were able to pick up many of the swimmers. General Harding and General Waldron made it to the beach on their own. But twenty-four men of the supply expedition were accounted dead and about a hundred had been wounded. In addition, at least twenty-eight natives had died. The heavy weapons and most of the reserve ammunition for the American attack on Buna had been lost, along with all rations and most of the medical supplies.

Notwithstanding this disaster, General Harding – still optimistic, and still anxious to get to Buna before reinforcements landed – ordered the attack to go forward at daybreak on November 19.

As planned, the 1st Battalion was to move up the coast on the right flank, the 3d up the inland trail on the left flank. Harding had counted on the Australians being in position to protect his left flank, pending the arrival of his 126th Infantry, then pushing forward toward Dobodura airfield; but he could not be sure of the Australians because he had lost radio contact with General Vasey. Therefore he ordered his 2d Battalion, then in reserve at Dobodura, to move out on the extreme left on the track that led to the Triangle at Buna.

In a drenching downpour on the morning of November 19, the troops on the coast started up the trail to Cape Endaiadere, two miles away. The autumn rains had set in; all aircraft were grounded; and the men were already beginning to feel the effect of the loss of the trawlers: their dinner the day before had been mainly rice and boiled papayas, and they carried only one day's rations and little more than a day's supply of ammunition. Yet they moved out laughing and joking, sure of an easy victory.

They were soon disillusioned. As they approached a coconut plantation just south of Cape Endaiadere, they were suddenly enveloped in a storm of machine-gun and rifle fire that seemed to come from everywhere and nowhere. Every movement drew a burst of fire from bunkers hidden in the thick jungle growth and high grass. As the day wore on, the Japanese outposts fell back a short distance, but the Americans, out of rations and with not much ammunition left, were in no shape to pursue. Bewildered by this unexpected setback, they ended the day badly shaken. And they noticed that the bodies of the few Japanese left on the field were not those of the 'sick Japs' they had been led to expect, but of healthy, well-armed soldiers.

On the left flank that morning, the 3d Battalion fared even worse on its inland trail. Rain made swamps of the area, so that the men had to move waist-deep and even chest-deep in water. When they slogged through to the narrow track between Old Strip and New Strip airfields, a blazing sun came out, but at the same time the men were met with such withering Japanese fire that they could make no further progress that day.

General Harding, shocked as he was by these developments, received another shock that evening. He was ordered by New Guinea Force to turn over to General Vasey the 2d and 3d Battalions of his 126th Regiment.

The order to give Vasey almost half of Harding's force was the result of a decision by General Blamey, with General MacArthur's approval, to make the main effort in the Australian sector of the advance, where there appeared to be a greater concentration of Japanese than in the American sector.

After the Australians had crossed the Kumusi River, General Vasey sent Eather's 25th Brigade down the left-hand track toward Gona and dispatched Lloyd's 16th Brigade down the right-hand track toward the main Japanese base at Sanananda. Ahead of both brigades were about 40 miles of track, from the foothills to the steaming tropical lowlands of the coastal plain, winding between thick jungle and flats of coarse yellow-green kunai grass, all shimmering in waves of humid heat.

Along the track to Gona, Eather's men saw signs of a hasty retreat, also installations that the Japanese had built and abandoned – large stables, and huts sheltering dumps of rice and barley – and evidences of the excellent work of the Japanese engineers in preparing roads, drains, and clearings. They encountered no Japanese, and were beginning to believe that Gona had been evacuated. Then, on the afternoon of November 18 in a kunai patch just south of Gona, they ran into intense rifle fire, some of it from snipers in trees, that pinned them down all that day and the next. With casualties mounting, not only from Japanese fire but from malaria, Eather's men withdrew after midnight on November 19, the sound of their movements covered by rain drumming on the leaves.

Lloyd's brigade, approaching Sanananda on the morning of November 20, came under heavy artillery fire from the Japanese main base, lost heavily, and was stopped.

CHAPTER IX

'TAKE BUNA'

'Our ground forces have rapidly closed in now,' asserted General MacArthur's communiqué on November 20, 'and pin the enemy down on the narrow coastal strip from Buna to Gona. We are fighting on the outskirts of both places.' The following day was the date General MacArthur had set for a simultaneous movement forward on the whole Gona–Sanananda–Buna front, in which 'all columns' were to be 'driven through to objectives regardless of losses.'

On the morning of November 21 came a message to General Harding: TAKE BUNA TODAY AT ALL COSTS. MACARTHUR.

Harding was astounded. His coastal force was pinned down by Japanese fire and his inland force was bogged down in swamps. He had just lost to the Australians most of his 126th Infantry – almost half his troops. The bulk of his supplies had disappeared when the trawlers were sunk, and since then, Japanese bombings and the delay in the opening of the airfield at Dobodura had made it impossible to make up the loss. On supply he was still, and was to remain for some time, on a 'hand-to-mouth, catch-as-catch-can basis'.

Nevertheless, his attack went forward on the morning of November 21.

At Cape Endaiadere his coastal and inland forces were soon stopped. Air attacks, from which much was hoped, were poorly co-ordinated. Twice that day American bombs fell on American troops, killing ten, wounding fourteen, and demoralizing many.

On Harding's extreme left, his 2d Battalion, 128th Infantry, which had just arrived in the Triangle area between Buna Village and Buna Government Station, moved out on the track toward Buna Station. Japanese fire from concealed machine-gun nests rained down on the track; and attempts to outflank it left the men floundering in deep swamps. Late that evening the battalion commander, Lieutenant Colonel Herbert A. Smith, radioed to Harding that he had run into strong opposition.

To bolster Smith's forces, General Harding asked the Australians to return to him a battalion of the 126th Regiment. They agreed, and General Vasey selected the 126th's 2d Battalion. These were the men who had made the killing march over 'Ghost Mountain', and were, therefore, in worse shape physically than any of the American troops; also, they had lost their commander, who had suffered a heart attack on the march and been evacuated.

The battalion seemed to have been marked out by fate for misfortune, and almost the worst stroke yet was the order to go to the Triangle, where the Japanese had constructed with bunkers an almost impregnable fortress protected on one side by Entrance Creek and on the other by neck-deep swamps. A minor but real element of mischance in being sent to this particular front was that young Major Herbert M. Smith, who had succeeded to the command of the battalion, had almost the same name as the commander he was to join, Lieutenant Colonel Herbert A. Smith. This inevitably led to confusion in radio messages.

On the plus side, both Smiths on this ill-starred front were to prove themselves energetic and imaginative leaders.

When Major Smith reached Colonel Smith's command post on the morning of November 23 at the Triangle, the two battalions were designated Urbana Force, to distinguish them from Warren Force on the coast. Colonel Smith as senior officer took command.

On the Sanananda front the commander of the U.S. 126th Regiment, Colonel Clarence M. Tomlinson, had been given by General Vasey the responsibility for leading the attack on November 22. The 16th Brigade had not made much progress on November 21 and had lost more than eight hundred men.

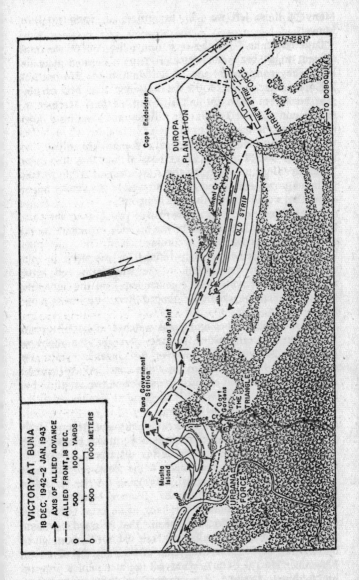

VICTORY AT BUNA
18 DEC, 1942–2 JAN, 1943
→ AXIS OF ALLIED ADVANCE
–– ALLIED FRONT, 18 DEC.

0   500   1000 YARDS
0   500   1000 METERS

Cape Endaiadere

DUROPA PLANTATION

Simeni Cr

OLD STRIP

NEW STRIP
WARREN FORCE

TO DOBODURA

Giropa Point

Buna Government Station

Gov't Gardens

THE TRIANGLE

Entrance Cr

URBANA FORCE

Musita Island

Buna

Many of those left were ill, exhausted, or weakened from hunger.

Ordered to hold for the time being, the Australians were content to sit back and watch Tomlinson's troops take the lead. They consisted of the 3d Battalion of the 126th and a 218-man detachment of the 1st Battalion that had become separated from its parent unit (destined for the Warren front) and wound up with Tomlinson. All these men had been flown over the mountains and looked fresh and healthy. Though they were short on food, they had plenty of cigarettes, which they generously passed around. They boasted that they had come 'to clean things up', advising the Australians that 'they could go home now'. Tomlinson envisaged a wide enveloping movement 'that would squeeze the Japs right out'.

Cheered by the arrival in his rear of two 25-pounder guns, Tomlinson moved out confidently in his wide enveloping movement. But things did not go according to plan. The Americans, who had not been adequately trained for patrolling in such country, became bewildered in the wild bush and scrub and lost contact with their commander. And the Japanese, far from being squeezed out, stopped them with heavy cross-fire.

This inauspicious beginning was watched at Port Moresby with deep concern, which became acute on the night of November 24, when a convoy of five Japanese destroyers was reported heading toward the Buna coast. Allied bombers sent out to intercept it claimed one sunk and two set afire; but Zeros drove the bombers off; and General Kenney admitted that some Japanese troops got ashore.

The following afternoon General Blamey and General Herring called on General MacArthur at Government House. Both Australian commanders were deeply disturbed. The Allies would have to bring reinforcements to the coast.

General MacArthur suggested bringing up the U.S. 41st Infantry Division from Australia. Blamey bluntly said he would rather put in more Australians, as he knew they would fight. Herring agreed. In the discussion that followed it became plain that both the Australian generals did not think much of the fighting qualities or leadership of the U.S. 32d Division. This was, General Kenney observed, 'a bitter pill for General MacArthur to swallow.' But he consented to fly to the battlefront the Australian 21st Brigade, which had been resting and training in Port Moresby.

An element in MacArthur's decision was his deep-down suspicion that the Australian generals might be right. General Kenney, who was staying at Government House, was convinced (though he still had little or no firsthand knowledge) that for ten days the American troops had been sitting around in the jungle doing nothing except worrying about the rain and the mud and listening to strange noises at night. He was willing to admit that they were green troops, tired and half-starved when they arrived at the front, and since then most had been suffering from dysentery and many from malaria; yet it seemed to him that their commanders did not seem to know what to do to get them moving. This argument appealed to MacArthur: the only commander at the front who had his entire confidence, General MacNider, had been wounded in the past few days and been succeeded by Colonel Hale, who was a National Guard officer and therefore suspect.

On the day following the conference with the Australians, Thanksgiving Day, General MacArthur ordered two of his operations staff officers to the front to find out what was wrong, Colonel Robert B. McBride, Jr., to report on Urbana Force and Lieutenant Colonel David Larr to observe Warren Force.

Colonel Larr arrived at the Warren front on November 27, on the heels of the complete failure of a Thanksgiving Day attack on Cape Endaiadere, and spent two days there. He saw that the troops were tired and listless, many of them ill. He talked to some of the War Department observers on the scene, whose judgment was that the troops had not been properly prepared for the shock of combat, and consequently would not keep going until they could close in with the enemy and kill him, preferring to stand off and attempt to kill at a distance with their rifles or have aircraft, mortars, or artillery do the job for them. He heard stories that men had on occasion thrown away their rifles, abandoned their machine guns, and retreated in panic into swamp or jungle.

On the basis of these observations, Colonel Larr reported to General MacArthur that the troops were not fighting.

What he apparently did not report was the real reason for the failure to 'take Buna'. The troops had not been provided with weapons that would defeat the Japanese bunkers. The bunkers were so cleverly concealed that they could not be spotted from the air, and were so close to the ground that shells from the 25-pounder guns would pass over them. Built of foot-thick coconut logs, they were impervious to rifle and machine-gun fire. They could be burned out with flame-throwers (as Marines at Guadalcanal were later to demonstrate), but the troops at Buna had no flame-throwers. Once in a while, a man could succeed in surviving the Japanese protective fire long enough to push a hand grenade through a bunker's firing slit, but as a commander on the scene later recalled, 'Many more failed than succeeded.' In such close-in attacks, tanks would have provided protection, but though General Harding was still trying to obtain tanks, none had been brought forward.

If Colonel Larr was aware of the impossibility of reducing the bunkers with the weapons at hand (there is no indication that he talked with General Harding) he may have thought it impolitic to stress a point that reflected, in the end, on G.H.Q.

His report concluded by criticizing commanders for operating too far to the rear. Here his criticism was justified. Colonel Hale's command post was at Hariko, a two-and-a-half-mile trek through the jungle from the front lines. General Harding's was at Embogo, eleven miles farther down the coast from Hariko.

Harding's journey to and from the front on Thanksgiving Day was hazardous and time-consuming. Shortly after midnight he embarked for Hariko on the trawler *Helen Dawn*, loaded with ammunition. On his night journey in the trawler he was accompanied by two sergeants, one of whom was E. J. Kahn, Jr., in peacetime on the staff of *The New Yorker* magazine. Though a full tropical moon shone down, under which Kahn felt 'somewhat conspicuous', no Zeros appeared; but shortly after three o'clock the *Helen Dawn* ran aground on a sand bar. She could not be dislodged. The general and his sergeants had to continue their journey in the ship's dinghy. Just before daybreak they were met on the beach at Hariko by a guard who was, according to Kahn. 'commendably imperturbable,' apparently seeing 'nothing odd in the patently curious circumstance that a Major General had arrived in his bailiwick at an unusual hour and in, of all things, a rowboat.'

General Harding got to the front lines in time to watch

the beginning of the attack on Cape Endaiadere, but had to leave before noon in order to walk back to Embogo before dark. Kahn noted that 'The long march home was featured by eleven river crossings. At one of these there was a rowboat, at other crude logs serving as bridges, at another a fairly respectable bridge built by the Engineers and bombed an hour or so after the general crossed it by the Japs, but at the rest there was nothing except water' – up to five feet deep, into which the general and his party plunged, sometimes removing their clothing, sometimes not bothering to. Tired from the long march, they were glad when a jeep appeared to take them the last half-mile home. They got there just before dark, in time for a Thanksgiving dinner of meat and vegetable stew made of C-rations, stewed onions, and weak coffee.

At his Embogo headquarters, far down the coast, General Harding felt it possible, at times, to forget about the war; it seemed to him that there was sometimes almost 'an air of rustic tranquillity' around the native huts under the trees – men shaving, taking baths, washing clothes, or going for a dip in the ocean.

But at the time of Larr's visit, Harding was already planning to move his command post closer to the scene of battle. The place he had selected was inland, near the airfield at Dobodura, which was almost equidistant from the Warren front on the right and the Urbana front on the left; trails led to both.

Harding needed to be closer to the Urbana front, particularly, where the two Smiths were still pinned down at the Triangle. At Colonel Smith's suggestion, Harding had ordered a change in the direction of the attack. Holding at the Buna Station impasse, the troops were to concentrate on Buna Village. By making a wide swing to the left, bypassing the Japanese bunkers, they would come out onto a wide grassy area from which they could move on the village. At the same time, because reports had indicated a lack of punch and 'some instability' among Smith's troops, Harding had ordered his own Chief of Staff, Colonel John W. Mott, to the Urbana front with instructions to take over the command if he thought the situation demanded it. Mott had lost no time in assuming command.

Three days after Thanksgiving, November 29, General Harding and his headquarters staff set out for Dobodura, a northwesterly trek of about 16 miles. Starting at 9 o'clock in the morning, the men made a leisurely march in the burning heat, stopping to rest, refresh themselves with coconut milk from coconuts thrown down from trees by native carriers, and, as they neared their destination at four o'clock, bathe in a river.

While Harding's party was on the march, a plane landed at Dobodura airstrip, discharged a passenger, and took off. The passenger was an Australian, Lieutenant Colonel W. T. Robertson, General Herring's senior liaison officer. Herring, who had opened an advanced headquarters behind the San-ananda front the day before, had sent him to find out what was happening on the American front.

Looking about him, Robertson saw no sign of life on the broad grassy airstrip until his eye caught a wisp of smoke curling up through the trees along the edge of the field. It came from a fire under a pot of stew which was being stirred, he saw to his surprise as he came nearer, by an American colonel. From the colonel he learned that General Harding was on his way up the track to Dobodura.

After some time had gone by, General Harding appeared. But he was unable to give Robertson much information on his infantry positions. He said he was quite out of touch with his forward troops and would be for some hours, since his headquarters Signal Corps operators had become so exhausted carrying the heavy divisional wireless set that they had left it in the jungle along the track, to be brought up later.

At this bit of news, Robertson was 'astonished and dismayed'; but he managed to conceal his feelings and merely said that General Herring would arrive at Dobodura the following morning. Sometime during the evening Harding learned that he would have a second visitor next day – General Sutherland, MacArthur's Chief of Staff.

When General Sutherland boarded the plane in Port Moresby next morning for the 45-minute flight to Dobodura, he was under orders from General MacArthur to inform General Harding of a major decision made the day before, based on Colonel Larr's very adverse report on conditions at the Warren front.

Larr's report had convinced MacArthur that something

would have to be done. His solution was to bring General Eichelberger of I Corps up from Australia to take control of the 32d Division. It was unusual enough for a corps to control one division only; it was bizarre in this case, when the 32d was not even a full division at the front, having committed only one complete regiment and part of another. But MacArthur's alternative to bringing in I Corps was to act through Hardin's Australian superiors, admitting in effect that they were right in their aspersions on American troops. Eichelberger was ordered on the night of November 29 to report at once to MacArthur.

This was the decision Sutherland was charged with conveying to General Harding. Landing at Dobodura in midmorning November 30, Sutherland found Herring there engaged in a discussion with Harding, the two generals and Colonel Robertson seated on ammunition boxes under the trees at the edge of the field. Harding was protesting at having lost Tomlinson's forces to General Vasey on the Sanananda front, and was insisting that his 127th Infantry Regiment, which had just arrived in Port Moresby, be brought to the Buna front. Herring did not think it either necessary or desirable to bring in more troops. Sutherland took Herring's side: he did not see how additional troops could be supported until reserve supplies had been built up at Dobodura.

The Australians departed around noon. Sutherland stayed for lunch. During lunch, Harding asked him whether the Australians were going to use his 127th Infantry on the Sanadanda front. Sutherland's reply was 'startling'. He said that Blamey preferred to use Australians, as he had a low opinion of the fighting qualities of the American troops. Sutherland also said that this opinion was borne out by Colonel Larr's report; and that, in consequence, General MacArthur had sent for General Eichelberger and would probably order him to the front. He wound up by asking Harding pointblank whether, in view of the lack of progress, he intended to relieve his top commanders, Colonel Mott on the Urbana front and Colonel Hale on the Warren front.

General Harding hotly defended his own troops. On the question of relieving their commanders, he was less positive. He knew that Colonel Mott had a 'notable talent for antagonizing superiors, subordinates, and contemporaries'; he also knew

109

that Mott was on bad terms with Colonel Larr; and as a long-time regular officer, he was no doubt well aware that (as Lieutenant General Lucian K. Truscott, Jr., put it in his memoirs) 'the military art is a most personal one.' Yet Harding pointed out that Mott seemed to be doing a good job in the few days he had been commanding Urbana Force. With regard to Hale, Harding frankly said that he questioned Hale's competence, but that he was 'doing fairly well in the only chance he had had to show his stuff.' Harding told Sutherland that he did not intend to relieve either Mott or Hale.

Sutherland returned to Port Moresby early in the afternoon and reported to General MacArthur on the day's conversations at Dobodura – doubtless including the remarks of Colonel Robertson, the Australian observer. He ended his report with a recommendation that General Harding be relieved at once on the ground that he insisted on keeping in command subordinates whose competence was open to question.

While Sutherland was making his report, General Eichelberger flew into Port Moresby from Australia with a small headquarters staff that included his Chief of Staff, Brigadier General Clovis E. Byers. He was met at the Seven Mile Airdrome by Colonel Larr, who told him that he would be given four or five days of briefings before he was sent to the Buna front. He and Byers were taken to quarters at Government House.

They had scarcely reached their rooms when they were abruptly summoned by General MacArthur. They found him striding up and down the long screened veranda. With him were General Sutherland and General Kenney. Kenney gave them a welcoming smile; but Sutherland's face was stern, as was MacArthur's.

Without preliminaries, MacArthur said that American troops had dropped their weapons and run from the enemy. He had never been so humiliated in his life. It was the kind of thing he would not stand for. He knew the troops had not been trained for jungle operations, that most were sick and all were affected by the climate, the burning heat and drenching rains; but he was convinced that a real leader could take these same men and capture Buna. Harding had failed and must take the blame for what had happened. He ordered Eichelberger to relieve Harding and his subordinate commanders or, he said,

'I will relieve them myself and you too.'

He stopped pacing long enough to look intently at Eichelberger. 'Go out there, Bob, and take Buna or don't come back alive.' Then, pointing to General Byers without looking at him, he added, 'And that goes for your chief of staff, Clovis, too.'

'Well, that was our send-off,' Eichelberger remembered later, 'and hardly a merry one.'

MacArthur said that though it would be desirable to give them four or five days of briefings, it would not be possible to give them even one day. Time was of the essence, for the Japanese might land reinforcements any day. Eichelberger and his staff were to leave for the Buna front in the morning.

Before noon next day Eichelberger was at the 32d Division command post near Dobodura. General Harding, disconcerted by the sudden arrival of the I Corps officers, was mystified by General MacArthur's instructions to Eichelberger to take command of the American troops at Buna. Harding was not sure what his own position now was; but he gathered from Eichelberger that General MacArthur was 'much dissatisfied' with the way things were going. In reply, Harding said the men were doing a good job under exceedingly difficult conditions and that his commanders instead of being relieved ought to be decorated.

Harding had just had good news from Colonel Mott on the Urbana front. In the early hours of November 30, Mott's men had gone clear through to the outskirts of Buna Village – the first breakthrough in the Japanese perimeter.

CHAPTER X

THE FIRST BREAKTHROUGHS IN THE JAPANESE DEFENSES

As soon as the black tropical night descended on the evening of November 29, men of the 126th Infantry's 2d Battalion (the 'Ghost Mountain' troops) began moving to the jump-off point for the attack on the open grassy field leading to Buna Village.

They moved slowly. There was no trail. It was hard for the men to find one another in the darkness, because they had no white cloth for armbands, not even cloth from underwear, for they had by then no underwear. Each man grasped the shoulder of the man in front of him and shuffled forward, the only guide the telephone wire leading to the jump-off point and the whispered advice of men in foxholes along the way. They moved forward with fixed bayonets, not yet permitted to fire.

A Japanese plane came over and dropped flares, but nothing happened until the column reached the jump-off point, the edge of the open kunai area. It was by then four o'clock in the morning, but still dark. Suddenly from a line of Japanese machine-gun posts, there erupted violent fire. 'Machine-gun tracers lit the entire area,' and 'there was more lead flying through the air . . . than it's possible to estimate, young Lieutenant Robert H. Odell later remembered. 'Everywhere men cursed, shouted, or screamed. Order followed order . . . Cowards crouched in the grass literally frightened out of their skins.'

This was the kind of fire that had been stopping the Americans when they tried to penetrate the beachhead. But this time the attackers let go with a concentrated burst of rifle fire – 'a solid sheet of flame,' Odell described it. 'Brave men led and others followed.' They kept going, crossed the kunai field, and reached the concealment of the jungle beyond – just in time, for by then dawn was breaking.

At the far edge of the field they overran a cluster of thatched-roofed houses made of timber and canvas, with wooden floors. When they entered the first house they smelled the sickly perfume the Japanese officers doused themselves with. On straw mats on the floor lay six officers.

What the Japanese thought when they awakened and became aware of a horde of shouting, cursing, ragged, bearded Americans will never be known, for they were all shot in their beds; one tried three times to rise before he was gunned down. Their orderlies had fled, leaving the breakfast rice still hot.

All around were evidences that the officers were marines who had been in China, the Philippines, and Java: beautiful watercolor prints, fine silks, and painted lacquer boxes. Other prizes discovered by the Americans were cans of meat, a welcome change from the Australian bully beef; and best of all, in a safe under lock and key, fourteen rolls of thin Japanese writing paper which the Americans assumed to be toilet paper, a great prize for they had not had any for weeks.

After stripping the buildings the men burned them, blew up the bunkers to which they were attached, and dug in. They expected counterattacks but none came; the only Japanese that appeared that day and the following night were a few snipers attempting to infiltrate back into their own lines.

Colonel Mott considered that a major breakthrough had been made in the Japanese perimeter, reporting to General Harding that the troops had gone clear through to the outskirts of Buna Village, overcoming 'a considerable area in which the Japanese defenders of the place had been living,' killing 'many Japs' and incurring 'fairly heavy casualties.'

This was the news Harding passed on to Eichelberger on his arrival December 1. Also, during the day an encouraging report on the Urbana front came from Colonel McBride, who had just returned from Mott's command post. Eichelberger, assuming command of all U.S. troops in the Buna area at one o'clock, ordered that Buna Village be captured that very night.

There was one dash of cold water on these plans. General Herring sent word by his Chief of Staff that he was not particularly interested in the capture of Buna Village; he wanted Buna Government Station.

Around midnight Colonel Mott telephoned General Harding to say that he had been prevented from capturing Buna Village that evening by a strong counterattack on the kunai field made by several large bodies of Japanese from Buna Station; however his lines had held, the Japanese had gone, and he intended to make a fresh attack on the village next morning. Eichelberger was called to the telephone. In some elation he told Mott he intended to give him a decoration, the Silver Star. He then informed General Herring of the counterattack.

Next morning General Eichelberger left for the front in a jeep, accompanied by General Harding and several other officers. After a while the bumpy coconut-log corduroyed road ended and the party went on foot through the blazing heat to Colonel Mott's command post. Just then the big guns in the rear opened up, heralding the beginning of the new battle for Buna Village.

At an aid station along the track where a number of men who appeared to be unwounded were sitting, some of them dozing under the trees, Eichelberger stopped to ask why they were not at the front. Most replied that they had been sent to the rear for a rest.

Arriving at the command post the generals found that Mott was at the front but had been notified that they were on their way. When he telephoned to warn them not to come forward because of the intense fire, he was told to return to the command post and soon appeared with Major Smith who, General Harding noted, was 'bearded like a member of the Army of the Potomac.' As they arrived, through the steamy jungle came the yells of men making a charge. Eichelberger congratulated Mott on the progress he was making.

But an hour or so later the news that came back to the command past was disappointing. The attack had been stopped at the bunkers in front of Buna Village. Eichelberger's misgivings were mounting. Sometime during the wait he had questioned Major Smith about the Japanese counterattack the evening before. Smith seemed surprised and said there had been none.

114

Suspecting that Mott's request that the generals not go up front was a ruse to keep him from finding out the true situation, Eichelberger set out for the front line, ordering Mott to stay behind. When he returned he was very angry. He had moved everywhere without being fired upon. Conditions at the front were deplorable, machine guns standing in the open without concealment, men unwilling to stir up enemy fire.

He was particularly incensed by three machine-gunners who for three days had not explored a side track because they believed that it was covered by a Japanese gunner. They still refused to do so even when Eichelberger offered to decorate any man who would go 50 yards down the track. He said that these men were cowards, he referred to the 'stragglers' he had seen at the aid station, and said that if he could find six brave men to go with him he could take Buna Village himself. He wound up with a sweeping assertion that the men had not fought.

At this point Colonel Mott, who had been under great strain and had had little sleep for two nights, lost his temper. Vehemently refuting the charge of cowardice, he emphatically defended the machine-gunners, the 'stragglers' (who he said were suffering from dengue fever) – and himself. When Mott had finished speaking, General Harding indicated his approval by demonstratively dashing his cigarette to the ground.

Major Smith remained silent. He thought that on the whole the men had fought well. He could understand that 'decorations look damn artificial to a soldier who is filthy, fever ridden, practically starved, living in a tidal swamp and frustrated from seeing his buddies killed.' It was also true that there were men in the aid station who were not wounded 'and there were men who did not relish attacking Japs in the jungle, and there were others who dodged fighting as long as they could.'

The trouble was, he believed, that Eichelberger had come to the front too early, before the men had become accustomed to combat. Smith was also charitable enough to take into account that this was the general's first combat command, and that he was under no little pressure himself.

Eichelberger returned to Dobodura convinced that the men were 'licked' and that something would have to be done. He knew that General MacArthur had spoken in anger when he told him to relieve Harding and that as corps commander he was under no obligation to do so. He called in his I Corps staff to advise him, describing the scene at Mott's command post. Unanimously they advised him to relieve Harding.

That evening General Harding came to Eichelberger's tent with a new plan to take Buna Village. Eichelberger listened absent-mindedly for a while and then began talking about what he had found at the front that was wrong. Harding took issue with him on one or two points; then, finally, seeing that he was making no impression, said, 'You were probably sent here to get heads, maybe mine is one of them. If so, it is on the block.'

'You are right,' Eichelberger replied, 'it was, and I am putting this man' – pointing to General Waldron – 'in command of the division.'

'I take it I am to return to Moresby,' Harding said, and Eichelberger said, 'Yes.'

Mott's relief was inevitable and Eichelberger had already decided to relieve Colonel Hale, even before the return, late that evening, of the two I Corps officers sent to inspect the Warren front, Colonel Clarence A. Martin and Colonel Gordon Rogers.

The two colonels had arrived at the Warren front in mid-afternoon, at a time when the fighting – which had been raging fiercely all day – had died down. As luck would have it, they were able to walk around without being fired upon, just as Eichelberger, who had appeared on the Urbana front during a similar lull in the battle, had been able to do. Martin and Rogers, therefore, after a visit of less than two hours, came to the same conclusion Eichelberger had come to, that the troops were not fighting.

Twenty-four hours later, Colonel Martin changed his mind. Sent to the Warren front to replace Hale, he made the discovery that the troops 'had little in the nature of weapons and equipment of what was normally considered necessary to dislodge an enemy from a dug-in, concealed position.' He concluded that even if he had found the men attacking vigorously on the afternoon of December 2, their attacks could not possibly have succeeded.

Eichelberger himself a few days later admitted that he had not known on December 2 what the troops were up against on the Urban front. Writing to General Sutherland, he praised the courage and will to fight of Harding's ragged, starving men, and assured Sutherland that General MacArthur could stop worrying about their conduct in battle.

But it was by then too late to save General Harding.

Harding flew back to Port Moresby on December 3. Early that afternoon, Lewis Sebring, who had returned several days before, saw him passing by the war correspondents' house in a jeep with his aide and Warrant Officer E. J. Kahn, Jr. At Sebring's shout the jeep stopped. Sebring expressed his amazement at seeing the general in Port Moresby.

'Well, Louis,' said Harding, 'I didn't take Buna.'

One of the men with him said, 'He's been relieved.'

The general smiled and the jeep moved on, leaving Sebring stunned and indignant. Later he made a note of the way Harding's staff felt: 'All want to go wherever he does. That isn't failure, and the faithfulness and loyalty of the men with whom he has been working is the best proof that Harding hasn't failed.'

That evening at the 32d Division's rear headquarters in Port Moresby, General Harding was informed by telephone that General MacArthur wanted to see him. At Government House (by then nicknamed the 'Ivory Tower') MacArthur greeted him cordially by his first name and proceeded to lift his spirits by telling him that his career would not be affected by what had happened; nothing would go on the record. MacArthur expressed no criticism; on the contrary, he said, in effect, that it was always the same with new troops, they had to learn in their first battle, and learn the hard way.

As to Harding's future, MacArthur wanted him to return to Australia on a month's detached service and at the end of it to report to him in person. He then chatted about the adventure in the *Minnemura*, and the swim, and ended by inferring that Harding was a sort of protégé of his – a reference to Harding's service at West Point when MacArthur was superintendent. 'Slightly dazed by this unexpected turn of events, and much relieved,' Harding boarded the plane for Australia, taking only the things he would need for a month's stay and leaving most of his possessions in Port Moresby.

He was never to return to New Guinea. His next orders, a month or so later, sent him back to the United States.

It was General Harding's misfortune, as it had been the misfortune of two Australian generals, Rowell and Allen, to be relieved just at the time when things were looking up. The completion of the airfield at Dobodura was the first step in improving supply, and the arrival of supplies that Harding had requisitioned some time before made it possible on December 3 for the troops at the front to have their first full meal in days.

On that day also, five armored Bren-gun carriers were landed at the Warren front, sent in lieu of the tanks Harding had requested from Milne Bay. The U.S. 105-mm. howitzer which he and General Waldron had been trying to obtain, and which was to prove momentarily (until its scanty supply of ammunition ran out) an effective weapon against Japanese bunkers, was emplaced behind the front on November 30. By that time a flight of small Australian Wirraway planes was available to aid the artillery in spotting its targets.

Eichelberger with MacArthur's backing was able to accomplish several things that Harding could not. Harding had been refused his 127th Infantry Regiment, but on December 3 General Herring promised it to Eichelberger. Herring also offered tanks and fresh Australian troops for the attack on the Warren front, an offer growing out of General Blamey's opinion (expressed confidentially to Prime Minister Curtin) that the Americans were not putting up a fight; his faith in them had 'sunk to zero'.

But the reinforcements could not come forward for some time, and Eichelberger, under pressure from MacArthur, was unwilling to wait for them. On the morning of December 3 he ordered an attack on Buna Village for the following morning, to be made by Major Smith's 2d Battalion of the 126th Infantry while Colonel Smith's 2d Battalion of the 128th staved off a counterattack from Buna Station.

That afternoon he sent General Waldron to the Urbana front to alert the troops. Waldron was accompanied by Colonel John E. Grose, the I Corps inspector general, who had just arrived from Australia to take command of the 126th Infantry. Eichelberger considered him 'a doughboy under his IG insignia, having had combat experience in the [first] World War.'

Inspecting his new command, Colonel Grose was shocked by the condition of the troops selected to make the attack. This was the battalion that had climbed 'Ghost Mountain'. In poor shape when they arrived on the coast, they had been badly shaken in the attack the day before, when they had not only come up against heavy Japanese fire but had been bombed and strafed by American planes and hit by American artillery. Some of the men had 'simply collapsed from nervous exhaution, crying like children and shaking from head to foot'. To Grose the visit to the troops was 'a terrible experience'.

He and Waldron asked Eichelberger to postpone the attack for a day, to give the men a little rest. Eichelberger agreed, though reluctantly. He had been encouraged by a report from the front that day that nine Japanese bombers – the great silvery planes flying so low that the Americans in their foxholes could see the faces of the pilots – had parachuted supplies on Buna Station, confirming his belief that the Japanese troops were not only tired and sick but were running low on supply. Also, he had a feeling that the Japanese were 'not in great force'.

For a strong combined attack on December 5 preparations went forward on the Sanananda Road as well as the Urbana and Warren fronts. General Eichelberger flew to General Vasey's command post on the Sanananda Road for a conference with Vasey, Herring, and Brigadier General Charles A. Willoughby of G.H.Q. on the plan for the attack in that quarter.

Five days before, a small party of Americans under Captain John D. Shirley had managed to get around to the rear of the advance Japanese position on the Sanananda Road, had overrun a Japanese camp, and established a defense perimeter astride the road. They had held it ever since, in spite of fierce Japanese attacks. It had become known as the Huggins Roadblock after Captain Shirley was killed and Captain Meredith A. Huggins, fighting his way to it with an ammunition and ration party, took command. The plan for December 5 was for an assault on the Japanese in the pocket created by the roadblock, to be made from two directions by the Americans of the 126th Infantry – under Australian command. Their commander, Colonel Tomlinson, returned to the Buna area with his headquarters on December 4.

The men who were to make the attack on Buna Village spent the day resting, cleaning their weapons, and cooking rice, having been given permission to light fires which had been hitherto prohibited for fear the smoke would alert Japanese snipers.

In the midst of preparations for the attack, a burly sergeant from Major Smith's battalion appeared at General Eichelberger's command post to ask a favor.

He was Staff Sergeant Herman J. F. Bottcher. Speaking with a German accent, he said he had come to America from Germany in the early 1930s because he was opposed to the Nazis and had taken out his first papers, but after a year at the University of California he had gone to Spain to fight with the Loyalists and had thereby lost his chance for American citizenship. He wanted citizenship badly, but none of his commanders in the 32d Division had been willing to help him. Eichelberger promised it to him if he did well in the coming attack on Buna Village.

The attack opened at ten o'clock on Saturday morning, December 5, with a bombing of Buna Government Station by nine B-25 bombers and a bombardment of Buna Village by artillery and mortars. For a moment there was a stillness, then with a whoop the infantrymen moved through jungle and swamp against the village on three sides. They were soon stopped cold by heavy machine-gun fire. In the center, one company managed to get within 50 yards of the village but suffered so many casualties that it could go no farther.

Early in the afternoon General Eichelberger, who had been at the front all day with Waldron and several other officers, decided to throw in Colonel Grose's only reserve, a badly battered company of Major Smith's 'Ghost Mountain' battalion. It was down to about eighty men, commanded by one of the two officers remaining, Lieutenant Odell. The lieutenant was given to understand that his men were to 'finish the job – actually take the Village' – and it was inferred that 'we needed little more than our bayonets to do it'. They started up the track toward the village but in minutes were 'definitely and completely halted' by withering fire that killed or wounded more than half the men.

Behind Odell's men, Eichelberger and several members of his party tried to go forward up the track. Sniper fire hit

General Waldron in the shoulder and so seriously wounded Eichelberger's senior aide, Captain Daniel K. Edwards, that doctors at a trailside hospital despaired of his life. Eichelberger, who had a father's affection for young Edwards, was 'full of grief' as he carried the young man back to the field hospital on a stretcher lashed to the hood of his jeep.

Soon after he returned to the rear the general had news of the one achievement in the day's fighting. Sergeant Bottcher, leading an eighteen-man platoon on the far right, had turned aside from the futile attack on the village, pushed north on a trail through the jungle, and by late afternoon had reached the edge of a stretch of beach between Buna Village and Buna Government Station, where he emplaced his one machine gun in the sand and dug in.

Reporting this breakthrough to General Sutherland, Eichelberger also reported another development – the birth of his own confidence in his tatterdemalion army: 'The number of our troops that tried to avoid combat today could be numbered on your fingers.'

The news from the all-out attack that day on the Warren front was depressing. The open Bren-gun carriers as they crawled over the uneven, stump-filled ground had been easy prey for the Japanese, who assaulted them with machine guns, hand grenades, 'sticky' bombs that stuck on the superstructures and an antitank gun. Within twenty minutes all five had been knocked out, the Australian commander had been wounded, and thirteen of the twenty crew members were killed, wounded, or missing.

The American troops attempting to support the carriers were blocked by fire from the Japanese log barricade near the coast and from hidden strongpoints in the coconut plantation; and the burning sun that morning took a heavy toll in heat prostration. Other elements of Warren Force attacking at both ends of the New Strip did no better. That night Colonel Martin was forced to report 'We have hit them and bounced off.'

The failure led to a decision by General Eichelberger to concentrate on the Urbana front, postponing an attack on the Warren front until the tanks and fresh Australian troops could be brought forward.

Bottcher's narrow strip between Buna Village and Buna Station, soon known as 'Bottcher's Corner', was assaulted from both directions at dawn on December 6, but Bottcher mowed the Japanese down with his machine gun. During the day he received a visit from the new commander of the 32d Division's forward troops, General Byers, who had taken over when Waldron was wounded.

Elated at the breakthrough, Byers had come to see what he could do to help Bottcher hold his hard-won position. He asked the men clustering around him, 'What do you need?'

In response, one of them turned a half somersault in the sand, exposing his naked buttocks. He was one of the diarrhea-stricken men on Ghost Mountain who had cut away the seat of their trousers.

'Pants,' he said. 'For God's sake, General, pants!'

Along with the pants Byers ordered reinforcements, a platoon from another company. Also, because the American line extended only to the edge of the beach, he sent up immediately a ten-man squad under Lieutenant Odell to break through to the sea.

On the gray sands of the beach, littered with the wrecks of Japanese barges, two pillboxes barred the way to the sea, one on the right only 15 or 20 yards away, the other a little distance down the beach on the left in the direction of Buna Village. No activity from either had been observed, nor was there any response when Odell threw a few grenades at the nearer pillbox. Suspecting that it was covered by an enemy machine gun, he half ran, half crawled to it, but no one fired. Inside he found a few Japanese soldiers, all either dead or dying.

Though the far pillbox was reinforced and could not be taken, Odell had achieved a narrow path to the sea, cutting off Buna Village from Buna Station.

The following morning – the first anniversary of Pearl Harbor – the sun came out after a night of drenching rain. Urbana Force launched a strong attack on Buna Village. It failed and provoked a counterattack from the Japanese at Buna Station who advanced on the right flank shouting their war cry – between a chant and a scream – heard by the Americans for the first time. The main counterattack was beaten off, but at heavy cost in casualties. Major Smith was severely wounded and had to be sent to the rear.

A charge on Bottcher's Corner that evening by forty or fifty screaming Japanese from Buna Station, trying to clear the beach so they could reinforce Buna Village, almost succeeded. It was repulsed, but by such a narrow margin that the Americans became 'jittery'; Odell began to shake all over and was unable to stop. In the blackness of the night the men could hear Japanese crawling toward them along the beach; these were dispatched with machine-gun fire, hand grenades, and even bayonets. Later that night Bottcher spotted a barge offshore moving toward Buna Village, black against the gleaming sea. He machine-gunned it and set it ablaze. A second barge towed it back toward Buna Station. No more boats appeared.

Just before daylight Odell, so exhausted that he was asleep standing up, was awakened by the arrival of reinforcements. Their first job was to bury the Japanese dead who were lying on the beach or were washed in and out with the tide, one of them an officer of high rank carrying a decorative sword. In the afternoon eighteen Japanese planes flashed by at about 300 feet, dropping supplies on Buna Station, but no more attacks occurred.

Bottcher had done well. On Eichelberger's recommendation he was commissioned a captain of infantry for bravery on the field of battle. Two years later, as a major, he was killed in combat in the Philippines. 'He was,' Eichelberger wrote long afterward, 'one of the best Americans I have ever known.'

While the beach at Bottcher's Corner was being cleared of the Japanese dead on December 8, the main body of the battalion launched another attack on Buna Village. Much was hoped from the use against the bunkers of the first flame-throwers, which reached the front that day. One was carried stealthily through the jungle to a point about thirty feet from a bunker on the southern edge of the village, but when the operator stepped out into the open and turned on the machine, all that came out was a dribble of flame extending not more than halfway to the bunker. It succeeded only in setting the grass afire and alerting the enemy, who killed the operator, two of the men covering him, and the Chemical officer in charge.

The fight for the bunker went on next day and by evening it was taken, but the Japanese still held Buna Village, and it was becoming evident that the 126th's 2d Battalion had become so depleted that it could do no more. The task of taking Buna

Village would have to be turned over to a battalion of the fresh 127th Infantry, which completed its movement to Dobodura on December 9.

That day electrifying news came from Gona.

CHAPTER XI

THE AUSTRALIANS TAKE GONA

On the somber black sands of the beach at Gona – from which Father Benson and the mission sisters had watched the Japanese warships on that fateful afternoon in July – the Japanese built strong pillboxes of the kind discovered by Lieutenant Odell at Buna, probably emplaced to repel Allied attacks by sea.

The pillboxes were discovered at Gona in late November in the course of an attempt to outflank the main Japanese defenses in the Gona Mission area, where Brigadier Eather's 25th Brigade had been effectively stopped.

The Australians swinging toward the beach through the swamps to the right of the mission were the veteran troops of the 21st Brigade, who had just been flown from Port Moresby back into battle: from planes winging over the mountains they had been able to look down on the narrow red thread of the Kokoda Track, over which they had plodded and crawled for two punishing weeks in the September retreat from Isurava. Their present commander, Brigadier I. N. Dougherty, was new to the scene, but most of the other officers were, like the men, veterans of the hard fighting in the mountains.

The commander of the lead battalion in the attack on the pillboxes was Lieutenant Colonel Hugh B. Challen, who had been Brigadier Potts's second in command. Challen had found out, during the mountain fighting, the need for commandos to harass the Japanese in their rear, and had organized a commando unit at Port Moresby, composed of three companies of picked men. Called Chaforce after Challen, the unit had been sent to the front in mid-October. But the Australian Command had not appreciated its possibilities and the unit had been broken up, one company allotted to each of Eather's battalions.

A Chaforce company under Lieutenant A. C. Haddy had since November 21 been protecting Eather's left flank west of Gona, a dangerous area where Japanese from Colonel Yazawa's mountain forces were trying to make their way southward down the coast from the mouth of the Kumusi River.

With Haddy holding on the left and Challen leading on the right, the attempt to outflank the Gona Mission position began on the afternoon of November 28.

As Challen's lead company, wading single file through a waist-deep swamp fringed with prickly sago palms, came out on the beach in the gathering darkness, the Japanese opened up with heavy fire from the pillboxes. All attempts to outflank the pillboxes failed, in the blackness of the night, and at last a continuous storm of fire drove Challen's battalion from the beach, badly crippled: of the eleven men killed, three were officers.

Next day Dougherty turned over the attack to a second battalion of the 21st Brigade, but it had no better luck that day or the next, though assisted on the second day by a fresh company of his third battalion led by an intrepid young commander, Captain J. H. O'Neill, aged twenty-two.

On the third day, December 1, as 25-pounder guns in the rear opened up on the Japanese defenses and mortar fire crashed down, young O'Neill and a party of eighteen men swept forward under cover of the mortar smoke and actually got into the central enemy position in the Gona Mission area, the men blasting their way in, firing machine guns from the hip and taking refuge in shellholes. But they were almost immediately assailed by Japanese fire from north and south, and hit by their own 25-pounder guns. Most of the men were killed. Captain O'Neill was mortally wounded. At last, the three or four who remained broke out to the west and crossed Gona Creek.

On the far bank they encountered men of Haddy's Chaforce company. The night before, at a coastal village a mile or so to the north of Gona (afterward known as 'Haddy's Village'), Haddy with part of his force had beaten off a strong attempt by the Japanese to reinforce Gona; but the past ten days in his exposed position had reduced his company of more than a

126

hundred men to less than fifty, and those who remained were gaunt and worn with strain and malaria. As darkness fell on the night of December 1, two of these men swam Gona Creek and from the Japanese side brought back dying Captain O'Neill.

Shortly after midnight three Japanese barges containing about two hundred of Yazawa's troops, moving down the coast from the mouth of the Kumusi River, tried to land near Gona but were driven off by Australian beach patrols; they continued toward Sanananda. Near daybreak the men on the beach saw flares lighting up the sky far out at sea and heard the sound of heavy bombing. It came from attacks by General Kenney's B-17s and B-25s on four Japanese destroyers coming from Rabaul with reinforcements. The destroyers were making for the Gona coast with about eight hundred troops, veterans of Indochina, commanded by Major General Tsuyuo Yamagata. Blocked by Kenney's bombers, the destroyers turned north and anchored at the mouth of the Kumusi River. Though Yamagata had suffered heavily in the bombing, he managed to put ashore about five hundred troops.

By December 2 the Australians also had a powerful reinforcement – the 39th Battalion, which had borne the full brunt of the Japanese invasion in July. Now fresh and rested, and fleshed out with about a hundred picked men, it was on its way to Gona as the lead element of the newly committed 30th Brigade. With it was its old commander, the resourceful and intelligent Lieutenant Colonel Honner.

The question was, how best to use the 39th? General Vasey was deeply concerned by the mounting cost of the battle for Gona. The 21st Brigade had in five days suffered battle losses of more than a third of its strength. Only Challen's battalion remained as an effective fighting unit; the other two battalions had been cut to pieces. Vasey became convinced that fresh troops might be wasted at Gona. He therefore went so far as to order Brigadier Eather merely to hold at Gona, aided by the two shattered battalions of the 21st Brigade formed into a composite battalion. The 39th and Challen's battalion were to march eastward down the coast to attack Sanananda.

Brigadier Dougherty, who had been placed in charge of the attack to the east, tried to carry out these orders on Demember 3, but found that the coastal track faded into impassable jungle and swamp. The men could not get through.

Vasey then revised his plans, instructing Dougherty to return to Gona with the 25th Brigade. In these rapidly changing plans there was, as the Australian historian of the battle has pointed out, 'more than a hint of bewildered desperation'.

Dougherty, spurred by a warning that the Japanese would probably land reinforcements at the mouth of the Kumusi River, got his troops in position for an attack scheduled before dawn on December 6, bringing his strongest battalion, Honner's 39th, south to a kunai patch below the formidable Gona Mission area to lead the attack, backed by Challen's men. The 21st's composite battalion was already in place on the beach ready to move westward toward the enemy's pillboxes.

In the darkness before dawn the attack began. The men on the beach reached the first enemy strongpoint but were stopped and could go no farther. Honner's main movement, on the left of the track toward a belt of timber – trees four or five feet in diameter with gnarled roots where the Japanese were dug in – got going under heavy smoke; but in the half light of early morning the smoke aided the defenders, who before they themselves could be seen poured out a heavy crossfire that killed twelve men and wounded forty-six, and stopped the offensive when it had gone only 50 yards through the kunai.

All the attackers gained that day, according to Honner, was 'fifty yards of useless kunai – and the knowledge that the enemy defense was no easy nut to crack'.

But events on the right of his main attack gave him hope that the defenses could be breached. Fighting patrols, covered by the noise and smoke of the initial onslaught, broke through outposts and almost succeeded in reaching the Gona Mission school (where Sister Mavis Parkinson had taught) before they were forced back into the slime of a sago swamp.

During the depressing night that followed, with pouring rain drenching the coast and flooding the swamps, there came to Brigadier Dougherty the alarming news that the Japanese were attacking Haddy's Village, weakly held by Haddy and his dwindling and fever-racked Chaforce troops.

As soon as Dougherty got the news, he sent to the rescue a fifty-man patrol of Challen's battalion. But it was already too late. Half a mile short of the village the patrol was stopped by a strong force of Japanese who had already taken Haddy's Village. The few Australians who had been able to escape from the village said that Haddy had ordered them to withdraw when he saw his position was hopeless. He had stayed behind to cover their withdrawal. Ten days later, after the village was retaken, Haddy's body was found under the native hut he had used for his headquarters; and the many Japanese bodies found around the hut showed that he had fought to the last.

By nightfall on December 7, Challen had joined his patrol, brought up the rest of his battalion, and formed a perimeter about a mile west of Gona.

That day an attack on Gona had been called off when Allied bombs began falling erratically; but preparations went forward for an all-out assault on the afternoon of December 8.

It was a last desperate gamble. Gona was becoming too costly. The number of effective fighters in Dougherty's four battalions, including Challen's troops on the track to Haddy's Village, was down to thirty-seven officers and 755 men – less than the normal strength of one battalion. His strongest battalion, the 39th, was needed at Sanananda. On the morning of December 8, Vasey warned Dougherty that this would be his last assault. If it failed, Gona was to be merely contained.

Honner, on whose shoulders fell the main burden of the attack, decided to make his main thrust with three companies on the right, where two days before his men had had some small success.

At 12.30 p.m. a concentrated artillery and mortar bombardment roared down on the Gona Mission area. Artillery shells equipped with delayed-action fuses, so that they burst nearly two feet underground, bored into the Japanese dugouts. Before the guns stopped firing, Honner's men on the right managed to creep up on enemy posts, so that they were in position to attack while the Japanese were still stunned by the underground concussions.

In this manner they quickly captured post after post, entered the area around the mission school, and created a wide breach for other companies to follow. By nightfall, the Australians had penetrated into the center of Gona. Only in the pillboxes on the beach and around the big trees on the left of the track did the enemy still hold out, and these strongpoints were soon reduced by determined, furious – and costly – onslaughts by the Australians.

All night, in an atmosphere 'strangely macabre even in that

ghastly place', the Japanese made desperate attempts to fight their way out through the Australian lines or reach the sea. Those who made it to the beach came under fire from the composite battalion; and if they tried to escape by running into the sea they were illuminated by the phosphorescence gleaming all around them, and were easily picked off. Elsewhere in the blackness of night there were the sounds of hand-to-hand combat – blows, panting breaths, shots, and screams.

On the morning of December 9, the 39th Battalion had linked up with the composite battalion on the beach and the battle had been won. As soon as Honner got a telephone wire into the mission area he sent back to Brigadier Dougherty the long-awaited message, 'Gona's gone!'

And yet, as the Australians that afternoon moved in to clean up the charnel house that Gona Mission had become, they were sobered in their moment of victory by what they saw. On the parapets of the dug-outs the Japanese had stacked their own dead as protection, and within they had used bodies as firing steps. In one bunker, rice had been stacked on corpses, and as more men had died lying on the rice, ammunition had been stacked on their bodies. The stench was so overpowering that the Japanese had fought in gas masks.

They still had plenty of ammunition, medical stores, and rice, though much of the rice was green with mold. Most impressive of all, the Japanese still had the will to fight, even after more than six hundred had been killed and they knew that their cause was hopeless. At one post on the beach during the mop-up that afternoon, nine wounded Japanese, all stretcher cases, opened fire on the Australians with grenades and rifles; and, next morning, out of the jungle charged a Japanese captain 'waving a samurai sword and roaring like a bull'.

The most important lesson of Gona, reported General Vasey, was the discovery that the Japanese soldier would 'fight to the death if that is in accordance with his orders'.

The Japanese last-ditch fighters had exacted a terrible price for the victory at Gona. When Brigadier Dougherty added up his losses on the morning of December 10, he found that the three battalions of his 21st Brigade had lost thirty-four officers and 375 men in battle (not counting casualties from malaria and deadly scrub typhus) and that additional battle casualties of six officers and 115 men had been inflicted on the 39th Battalion. These losses represented more than 41 percent of Dougherty's strength. And the figures did not tell the whole story. Aside from the cost in human suffering, from a military point of view the men lost at Gona were irreplaceable, for they were for the most part battle-wise veterans, veterans moreover who had had a chance to rest and retrain.

In the light of these casualties, it appears that General Vasey might better have stuck to his plan to contain the Japanese in their bunkers and pillboxes at Gona and leave them to starve, contenting himself with holding back the Japanese reinforcements trying to move southward from the Kumusi down the coast.

At the time Dougherty counted up his losses, he had already ordered Honner to join Challen in retaking Haddy's Village, and on the morning of December 10 the 39th Battalion plodded northwestward through inland jungle and swamp to form the left prong of a pincers movement on the village, while Challen's men formed the right prong on the coast.

Early on the following afternoon the men of the 39th came up against Japanese outposts at the village. They were stopped by a storm of fire. From that time on, for the men on both prongs of the attack it was a matter of edging slowly forward, day after day, against determined opposition by Japanese troops who, captured documents revealed, had recently landed. Not until the morning of December 18 did the Australians overrun Haddy's Village. In the week's fighting they had suffered 129 casualties, of which most were borne by Honner's battalion — two officers and 105 men.

But they had dissolved what could have been a major threat to the Australians and Americans on the Sanananda and Buna fronts.

CHAPTER XII

THE IMPATIENCE OF THE GENERALS

A week after being dispatched to the front to 'take Buna' General Eichelberger was begging General MacArthur to be patient.

Unwilling to risk again the heavy losses that had been incurred on December 5, Eichelberger was not spurring the 127th Regiment to make immediately an all-out attack on Buna Village. On the Warren front, a fresh offensive had to await the arrival of tanks, sent up from Milne Bay in freighters and put ashore in the first landing craft to reach New Guinea – six 'Higgins boats' (forerunners of the L.C.V.P.). The tanks were to be manned by Australian crews, and the weary Americans in the area were to be augmented by fresh Australian troops brought up from Milne Bay, men of the 18th Brigade who after winning the first victory in New Guinea had remained at Milne resting and training. Their big, burly, competent commander, Brigadier George F. Wootten, was to assume command on the Warren front. All this took time.

On the Sanananda front, General Vasey also needed a respite. The December 5 attack by the Americans of the 126th Regiment on the Japanese pocket at the Track Junction south of Huggins Roadblock had been stopped, with heavy casualties; and an Australian effort two days later had also been costly and ineffective. At the roadblock, the Americans crouching in their foxholes under broiling sun by day and drenching rain by night, tormented by thirst and hunger and depleted by Japanese forays, were still holding, but were almost at the end of their endurance.

As a result of these frustrations in the first two weeks of December, General Herring and General Eichelberger were in agreement that 'we must go forward yard by yard', pending reinforcements. They were gambling that the Japanese would not succeed in reinforcing their beachhead; and that General MacArthur would remain patient.

But the generals at higher headquarters in the rear, Japanese as well as American, were thirsting for victory. The impatience of General MacArthur in Port Moresby was matched by the impatience of General Adachi in Rabaul.

Lieutenant General Hatazo Adachi, Chief of Staff of the North China Area, arrived in Tokyo in mid-November to take command of the Japanese 18th Army, newly formed for operations in New Guinea.

For Adachi, an ambitious officer with a tense face adorned by a thin mustache, this was a promotion, and he was determined to make good in his new assignment; moreover, he was instructed by Premier Hideki Tojo himself, fresh from an audience with the Emperor, that he was to stop the enemy's advance in New Guinea at all costs. In this effort he was to operate under Lieutenant General Hitoshi Imamura, conqueror of Java, who had just been given command of the 8th Area Army, a new organization comprising not only Adachi's army but the 17th Army in the Solomons. Imamura, a plump general with a reputation for brilliance, was directed by Tojo to recapture Guadalcanal – his first priority – and to hold and consolidated at Buna while preparing for future operations, presumably against Port Moresby.

A few days later Adachi took off for Rabaul with his headquarters staff, the party traveling in four flights of seaplanes. Making overnight stops in Saipan and Truk, they crossed the equator, drank a toast in beer, and headed into the Southern Hemisphere.

Approaching Rabaul at sunset on November 22, they had a veiw of blue harbor surrounded by volcanoes belching smoke and ringed by coconut palms, red poinciana trees, and jungle. The seaplanes settled down on the water in the midst of the ships of the Southeast Area Fleet. As soon as the officers got ashore that evening, sirens began to wail and everyone took to air-raid trenches. All night long, the Allied bombers came and went; bombs fell around the ships in the harbor and the ground rumbled as if from an earthquake.

Adachi was gratified to find that fresh troops to reinforce New Guinea had arrived in Rabaul from Indochina, commanded by General Yamagata. The first echelon – a battalion of infantry and a company of mountain guns, accompanied by Yamagata – left Rabaul in four destroyers on the night of November 27, but was turned back next day by Allied bombers, which damaged two ships. The second echelon, quickly loaded, was on its way the following evening. These were the troops under Yamagata that came under air attack near Gona, turned north, and were landed at the mouth of the Kumusi River on December 2.

A third lot of reinforcements, again a battalion of infantry and a company of mountain guns, left Rabaul in six destroyers on December 7. In this convoy was Major General Kensaku Oda, who had come from his post as superintendent of the Toyohashi Reserve Officers' College in Japan to be General Horii's successor as commander of the South Seas Detachment; Oda had orders to report to Yamagata at the mouth of the Kumusi. But again, Allied bombers forced the ships back to Rabaul.

In the days following this setback, anxiety mounted in Rabaul over the fate of the troops at Gona, with whom contact had been lost. On orders from Adachi, General Yamagata sent one of his staff officers down the coast by barge to see what he could find out. He reported that there had been no sign of fighting at Gona since December 8. Hoping that its defenders had been able to withdraw to the main position at Sanananda, he proceeded there, but found that Colonel Yokoyama knew nothing.

The loss of Gona, which had been defended by picked troops from Formosa, considered excellent jungle fighters, was extremely serious. Moreover, from Sanananda Colonel Yokoyama continued to appeal for food and medicine for his men. Many were dying from disease and malnutrition. A report from him on December 11 was so gloomy that Adachi's staff could hardly believe it.

At this point General Adachi became so alarmed that he made up his mind to go to New Guinea and lead his troops in person. When his staff tried to dissuade him, he argued, 'If I don't go, who will save the Buna Detachment?' It was his only battlefield unit. He said, 'I am not going to look on while my only son is killed in battle.' But he was ordered by General Imamura to remain in Rabaul.

A fourth try at reinforcing the beachhead was decided upon, to be the last attempt; the Japanese Navy, appalled by the loss of destroyers, made that plain. Instead of attempting a landing at the Kumusi, the landing was to be made about 30 miles up the coast at the mouth of the Mambare River. The force of eight hundred men that had been turned back on December 8 left Rabaul on December 12, accompanied by General Oda. Next day, when off Madang, the convoy was spotted by Allied bombers but escaped in a thunderstorm and in the early hours of December 14 Oda's troops got ashore at Mambare Bay.

The Japanese destroyers had come prepared for a quick get-away, their decks stacked with small landing barges and water-proof cases of supplies, to which buoys were lashed. In the darkness the troops went ashore in the barges, the supplies were dropped over the side, to be washed in by the tide, and the destroyers pulled out. Before daybreak the troops got most of the supplies ashore and dragged them and the barges to the shelter of the jungle – just in time, for shortly after dawn Allied planes came over and bombed the beaches.

Though Oda doubtless had been warned that New Guinea was 'a dark, uncivilized place,' he could hardly have imagined anything more savage than the mouth of the Mambare River. Beyond nipa palms along the muddy banks stood grotesquely shaped mangroves whose gnarled, twisted roots rose out of the oozy mud. Through the thick jungle, which the sun never penetrated, creeks made tunnels and in their black waters crocodiles lay.

And on the morning of the landing the jungle hid a human enemy – a young Australian 'coastwatcher', Lieutenant Lyndon C. Noakes. At his camp nearby he had been awakened by the bombing. Making his way quietly through a swamp to the Japanese encampment, without being detected he fixed the position of the tents and dumps in relation to a sandy beach easily seen from the air and sent the information back to headquarters by wireless. Next morning the bombers returned and struck at Oda's supplies with deadly accuracy.

The Japanese tried shifting their dumps, but again Noakes spotted them, reported the new positions, and the bombers returned. Most serious were the losses in the landing craft, which had been depended upon to take the troops down the coast.

Deliverance from this unhappy spot came to Oda a day or so later when a big landing barge chugged into the river mouth, operated by a member of a Japanese 'shipping engineer unit', based on the Kumusi River, who had been dispatched by Yamagata to look for Oda. With the help of the big barge and the use of the small landing craft that remained, Oda with as much of his force as could be crammed aboard was soon on his way down the coast. Hugging the shore and moving only at night, on December 18 he arrived at Yamagata's headquarters about five miles northwest of Gona.

Reporting to Yagamata, who was his superior in rank, Oda found him in a desperate state. He had been pressing toward Gona, capturing Haddy's Village and attempting to send his men beyond it, but after the fall of Gona the Australians had blocked him and cost him so many casualties that he was unable to do more. Therefore Yamagata needed the men Oda had brought down the coast.

Leaving them behind, Oda and his staff proceeded by barge to the main Japanese concentration near Sanananda, reaching there on December 21. Oda at once took over command from Colonel Yokoyama.

The escape of Oda's convoy from the bombers on December 13 so alarmed General MacArthur that he immediately wrote a strong letter to General Eichelberger, insisting that he attack Buna Village at once, before the Japanese reinforcements could make their presence felt at the beachhead. 'Time,' he warned, 'is working desperately against us.' The tone of the letter showed that his patience was wearing thin.

While the letter was being written, Eichelberger was directing an advance on Buna Village to take place the following morning. He had not informed General MacArthur of it because he 'did not want to get the Chief's hopes up'.

Early on the morning of December 14, after a heavy bombardment by 25-pounders and 400 rounds of mortar fire, the troops of the 127th Infantry attacked. There was no response from the enemy. Moving cautiously, fearing a trap, the infantrymen entered Buna Village at ten o'clock to find that the Japanese had gone.

They had, in fact, evacuated the village on the night of December 13. Most of the hundred men who had been holding it managed to make their way by sea west to Sanananda or east to Buna Station. They left behind only a few guns, some ragged clothing, and a small stock of canned goods and medical supplies. The thatched huts in the wrecked, empty village had been blown to bits, the coconut palms splintered; there was a mass of wreckage. Significantly enough, the bunkers, though they bore evidence of direct hits by the 25-pounder guns, still stood.

The unopposed occupation of this shambles was magnified by General MacArthur's headquarters into a major victory. Under a screaming lead headline in the New York *Times* of December 15, ALLIES TAKE BUNA IN NEW GUINEA, the official communiqué asserted that American troops, 'scoring their first major offensive victory over the Japanese for General Douglas MacArthur, captured Buna Village yesterday.'

Nowhere on the front page that day was there any mention of the main objective, which was Buna Government Station, the place that gave its name to the campaign on the New Guinea coast. Toward the end of the story, buried on a back page, was the admission that Buna Government Station was 'still holding out'.

D-Day for the attack designed to encircle and capture Buna Government Station was set at December 18.

On that day Brigadier Wootten and his Australians with tanks, supported by the American elements of Warren Force, were to move forward on the right to take Cape Endaiadere, then cross the bridge over Simemi Creek between New Strip and Old Strip and advance northwestward toward Buna Station.

Urbana Force, moving northeastward on the left, also had a water barrier to cross, Entrance Creek. The Japanese had strong fortifications on its banks, the strongest, honeycombed with bunkers, in the area the Americans called the 'Triangle', where the track to Buna Station branched off from the track to Buna Village.

As Entrance Creek neared the sea it became an estuary, separated from the sea by sand spits and containing a crescent-shaped island (Musita Island) on the land side. Colonel Tomlinson, the new commander of Urban Force, planned to clear Musita Island, then reduce the Triangle and launch his attack on Buna from the high ground where once had flourished the Government Gardens.

In preparation for Brigadier Wootten's attack on Cape Endaiadere eight tanks began to grind toward their assembly area after sundown on December 17. Following the tanks, about five hundred Australians made their way through the fading light to their own assembly area. During the night while some tried to sleep in the undergrowth or talked quietly, patrols crawled forward to locate enemy strongpoints.

The Americans on this front, commanded by Colonel Martin, were in reserve, their mission to hold in the area around New Strip.

At first light on December 18 seven tanks (one remaining in reserve) and the Australian troops began to move toward the start line. Approaching it the men saw a rusting Bren carrier, a reminder of the ill-fated attack on December 5. Beyond, rows of tall coconut palms of the Duropa Plantation marched down to the sea, ghostly in the dim light of early morning. At their base in the thick kunai grass were hidden the long bunkers that had so long barred the way to Cape Endaiadere.

The morning was cloudy, so that no bombers came over to help, but at 6.50 an artillery bombardment roared out from the rear. Ten minutes later the guns stopped and even as the smoke was billowing away through the palms the Australians went forward. They attacked in three columns, two companies on the right with tanks through the plantation where the ground was firm, the third company without tanks turning left toward the grassy, marshy area around New Strip.

The tanks, lightly armored and designed for speed (they could do 40 miles an hour) moved slowly so as not to outstrip the men who strode beside them. Throttled down to the speed of a walking man, they seemed 'like race horses harnessed to heavy ploughs'; moreover, they were almost blind in the thick high grass. But guided by the infantrymen they were able to destroy machine-gun nests that had hitherto defeated men unprotected by armor, and to get close enough to bunkers to blast out the defenders with their 37-mm. guns. Another use for this gun was soon discovered: it could cut through tree trunks and bring snipers crashing to the ground.

The Australian infantrymen were superb. Walking upright, some with leaves stuck in the mesh covering of their 'tin hats' like gay cockades, they moved steadily forward with Tommy guns blazing, closing in on bunkers to hurl grenades through the openings, and as they marched they beat the underbrush for snipers – a lesson they had learned at Milne Bay.

In the dash and momentum of this determined attack, a platoon and one tank on the extreme right near the beach defeated Japanese post after post and by eight o'clock, only an hour after the jump-off, reached the coastline beyond Cape Endaiadere.

The Japanese, recovering from the shock of the unexpected attack, began to fight back violently, some of them with Australian Bren guns. The defenders were the cream of the Japanese forces on the Buna coast. Most of the thousand men defending Cape Endaiadere were the 229th Infantry's veterans of Sumatra; and they were ably led by Colonel Hiroshi Yamamoto.

When the rest of the tanks came up, the Japanese sprayed them with machine guns, threw incendiary bombs against their sides, and lit fires under them when they stalled against stumps. As the leading tank officer was peering through his vision slit, a Japanese jumped on his tank, thrust his rifle against the slit, and fired. Bullet and steel splinters gouged the Australian's face. Only two tanks were burned out, however, and the coastal columns gradually routed the enemy.

The column heading for New Strip without tanks ran into such heavy fire from a cluster of strongposts that it was stopped in less than ten minutes. After an advance of only a hundred yards, the company lost forty-six out of eight-seven men. In an attempt to infiltrate, a platoon was sent out and every man was killed. The Americans tried to help, crawling forward in the tall grass, but could get no closer than 30 yards to the beleguered Australians.

An appeal went out for tanks. At one o'clock three appeared, and a desperate plan was worked out for a tank-infantry attack. An hour later it began. Infantrymen accompanying the tanks fired Very lights to indicate the targets; others sprayed the trees with Bren guns. As the Very lights streaked into the bunkers, the tank shells followed. Bunkers blazed high when their dry coconut logs caught fire, and the Japanese ran out screaming.

By three o'clock it was all over. All sixteen of the bunkers had been cleaned out or abandoned. The Australians, with the Americans mopping up behind them, held the eastern end of New Strip.

By nightfall on December 18 the coastal area from New Strip on the south to a point about 500 yards west of Cape Endaiadere on the north had been wrested from the Japanese. Casualties had been heavy, some eleven officers and 160 men, more than a third of the attacking strength.

General MacArthur's communiqué announced a major victory.

And yet, as the New York *Times* correspondent on the scene that day reported, the fight for Buna was far from over.

CHAPTER XIII

PUSHING ON TO VICTORY
AT BUNA

On the morning of December 24, General Eichelberger sent General MacArthur a Japanese officer's sword as a Christmas present. Dispatching the sword, he was hoping with all his heart that before the day was over he could present his general also with a victory.

For the past week the advances of Buna Government Station by both flanks, Warren Force on the right and Urbana Force on the left, had been painfully slow. Both commanders, Brigadier Wootten and Colonel Tomlinson, had to cross unfordable streams to get to Buna, Wootten the broad, sluggish Simemi Creek, overflowing its banks into soggy marshes, Tomlinson, deep, tidal Entrance Creek.

Brigadier Wootten's only hope of getting his tanks across Simemi Creek was a 125-foot log bridge spanning creek and swamp between New Strip and Old Strip; but Colonel Yamamoto in his withdrawal to the far side had blown a large gap in it. Also, Yamamoto after setting up his headquarters and siting big guns at the creek's mouth (the only place it could be forded), had manned bunkers on Old Strip that dominated the bridge. Until these bunkers could be reduced, men could not get out onto the bridge to repair it.

Days went by while the Australians probed the bank downstream to find a place where infantrymen could ford the creek and neutralize the bunkers. The most promising place appeared to be a spot just northeast of Old Strip, but on the morning of December 22 the leader of the search party, Captain R. W. Sanderson, was forced to admit failure.

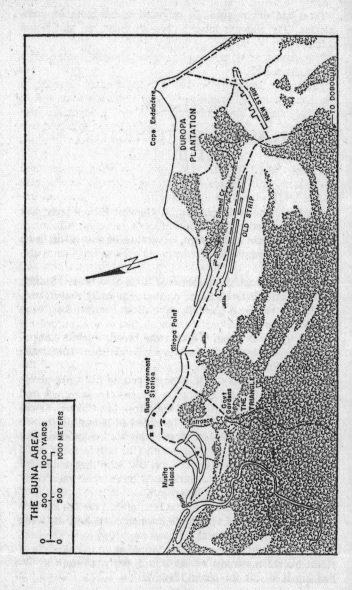

THE BUNA AREA

0 ___ 500 ___ 1000 YARDS
0 ___ 500 ___ 1000 METERS

Cape Endaiadere

DUROPA PLANTATION

NEW STRIP

TO DOBODURA

Siment Cr.

OLD STRIP

Giropa Point

Buna Government Station

G. Govts CT.

THE TRIANGLE

Entrance

Musita Island

Buna

Tired and discouraged, he reported to his battalion commander, 'My platoons have probed all night, sir, and found nothing.'

'You know what to do when your platoon commanders can't finish a job!'

Thereupon Sanderson walked into the swamp. Covered by two Bren guns, he waded and swam for some time and at last came out on dry, flat ground. He saw a galvanized iron hut on legs, which looked like a control tower, glimpsed two Japanese running into the jungle beyond, and realized he was on Old Strip.

The rest of his battalion followed him during the day, and by the morning of December 23 were in the rear of the bunkers in the bridge area. As they approached, the Japanese unaccountably fled. By noon the bridgehead on Old Strip had been neutralized.

Since daybreak a platoon of American engineers had been putting down coconut-log flooring over the gap in the bridge, working all morning under fire. Shortly after noon they had a catwalk down and two American battalions began running across. By nightfall all were in place beside the Australians. The tanks were to follow as soon as the bridge was strong enough to take them.

Early on the morning of Christmas Eve four tanks clanked across the log bridge. These were the last serviceable tanks Brigadier Wootten had on hand, all that were left of the original eight. He was reluctant to commit all of them, because he knew that the Japanese on the far bank had antiaircraft guns that could fire on tanks and knock them out. But as these guns had been silent for several days, he persuaded himself that they were either out of ammunition or had been destroyed by artillery fire.

The tanks moved out abreast, 50 yards apart, up the kunai-covered strip in the blazing morning heat, followed by the Australian and American infantrymen. For half an hour, all went well. Then the tank commander on the extreme left saw a flash, felt a hit, and the side of his tank seemed to split. He tried to warn the other tanks.

'Get out! The ack-ack gun's operating!'

But his radio was not working. In a matter of minutes the gun knocked out the other three tanks, killing two of the tankers, mortally wounding another, and badly wounding two more, one of whom lost a leg. The big enemy guns continued to fire down the center of the strip. Snipers fired from the jungle right and left. The infantrymen were stopped after an advance of not much more than 500 yards up Old Strip, and no more gains could be made that day.

On the Urbana front, the problem presented by an unfordable stream was even worse. Entrance Creek was spanned only by a footbridge that led directly into the formidable Triangle bunkers. By December 21, attacks using this bridge had proved so costly that General Eichelberger decided to bypass the Triangle and cross the creek at a point about 400 yards downstream opposite Government Gardens, where he intended to launch his Christmas Eve attack.

Arriving at the crossing site in midafternoon, the men of the company which was to lead the attack found that the creek was 50 yards wide. Wading out into it, they discovered that the water was over their heads; moreover, enemy fire poured down upon them; one man was almost blown out of the creek by a grenade. The tide was coming in, the water lapping over mangrove roots on the bank, and the current was running swift.

To the company commander, Captain Alfred E. Meyer, a crossing there in broad daylight seemed suicidal. He pleaded with Colonel Grose (who by then had succeeded Colonel Tomlinson as commander of Urbana Force) to let him wait until dark. Grose had already asked Eichelberger for more time; but the general, 'most impatient'. had refused.

Grose replied: 'Captain Meyer, you will cross your company here and now and that is an order.'

Time after time, swimmers were turned back by enemy fire. Several drowned. By nightfall Meyer had obtained from the engineers a piece of heavy rope. Holding onto it, most of his company got across that night, but the crossing had cost six men either shot or drowned. Those who reached the far bank found themselves trapped in a narrow bridgehead by enemy fire that cost eight men killed and forty wounded. When the rest of the company crossed with the follow-up company next day on a footbridge constructed by the engineers upstream, they saw bobbing in the creek the bodies of the men drowned the day before.

General Eichelberger, taking great satisfaction in making 'troops in their first fight cross an unfordable stream in the face of the enemy in the dark,' had his bridgehead in Government Gardens; and on December 22 and 23 good news came from Musita Island. The arrival of six Australian assault boats had enabled engineers to put down a pontoon bridge from the mainland to the south shore of the island. Troops ran over the bridge, cleared the Japanese from the island, and discovered on the north shore a Japanese footbridge, rickety but still usable, that led directly into Buna Station.

The discovery of the Japanese bridge came too late to change the direction of the Christmas Eve attack, but it did make possible a twenty-man feint from the island to Buna during the attack, to throw Captain Yasuda's Buna garrison off balance. Also, the men on the island had, for harassing fire, two 37-mm. guns firing canister – old-fashioned ammunition consisting of small pellets which were surprisingly effective in the jungle.

'I think we are going places,' Eichelberger wrote MacArthur.

On Christmas Eve morning the assault companies moved out into Government Gardens under a rolling artillery barrage, from the rear, and massed mortar fire from Entrance Creek directed by Colonel Melvin McCreary (Eichelberger's Artillery officer), perched high in a coconut tree. Ahead of them, the Gardens, neglected and overgrown with shoulder-high kunai grass, extended for about 400 yards. Then a narrow swamp had to be waded to reach the objective, a mile-long stretch of coconut plantation on the coast between Buna Station and Giropa Point, which was, Eichelberger believed, the heart of the Japanese position.

Almost as soon as the attackers left the line of departure, they were enveloped in Japanese fire – from Yasuda's artillery, from snipers in swamp trees, and, worst of all, from deadly bunkers hidden in the kunai. Before ten o'clock the lead company on the right was cut to pieces. Soon the company on the left, and the follow-up companies as well, were pinned down. The platoon from Musita Island did manage to get across the Japanese bridge and into Buna Station, but after losing eight men killed was forced back to the island. At the end of the day the advance into Government Gardens had gained no more than 150 yards.

For General Eichelberger, the news of the failure of the attack was a bitter blow. Toward evening he also learned that Colonel McCreary, who could ill be spared, had been badly wounded: struck in the back by a shell fragment, McCreary had strapped himself to his tree and continued to direct the mortars until he lapsed into unconsciousness from loss of blood and had to be evacuated. All in all, Eichelberger reported to General MacArthur, Christmas Eve was the 'all time low' of his life.

Colonel Grose asked for time to reorganize, and staff officers advised against another attack on Christmas Day, but Eichelberger was determined to force it. It was, it seemed to him, the hardest decision he ever made in his life – and yet in a way it was easy, for he suspected that the fiasco the day before had brought him perilously close to being relieved.

This time he went to the Urbana front to direct operations in person. The day began somewhat better; one company blasted its way through the gardens and succeeded in reaching the swamp area near the coconut plantation on the coast. But these men were soon cut off from the rest of the troops. No other gains could be made through the storm of fire poured down by the enemy. Eichelberger's Christmas dinner, a cup of soup and a cup of coffee given him by a doctor at a trailside hospital, had been shaken out of his hand by a Japanese mortar barrage.

Returning to his command post that evening, thoroughly disheartened, he found there an ominous visitor, General Sutherland. He said that General MacArthur was being needled by the Australian generals, who could not understand why the Americans, who were believed to outnumber the enemy, had not made more progress.

Also waiting for Eichelberger was a letter from General MacArthur, thanking him for the sword, and offering – from his 'Ivory Tower' in Port Moresby – a word of advice: the fighting at Buna was being done with gallantry but with too little concentration of force. 'Where you have a company on your firing line, you should have a battalion; and where you have a battalion, you should have a regiment. And your attacks, instead of being made by two or three hundred rifles, should be made by two or three thousand . . .

'I beg of you to throw every ounce of energy you have into carrying out this word of advice from me, as I feel convinced that our time is strictly limited and that if results are not achieved shortly, the whole picture may radically change.'

In reply Eichelberger could only point out that he was throwing into the front line all the fighting strength he had. 'I hope you will not let any Australian generals talk down their noses at you.'

Eichelberger might have been comforted if he had known that in far-off Tokyo the Emperor of Japan was giving a 'word of advice' to Army Chief of Staff Sugiyama. His Imperial Majesty had heard that the enemy had tanks at Buna. 'Don't we have any tanks in this area?'

In the jungles of Guadalcanal and Buna, Japanese front-line commanders were in despair at the ill-informed impatience of their superiors in the rear, feeling deeply that 'The big shots' in Tokyo 'should come out here and see what we have to take and then they might understand!'

On Christmas Night a Japanese submarine surfaced off Buna Station, unloaded rations and ammunition, shelled the shore, and quickly submerged to escape the American PT boats that were nightly on the prowl along the coast.

The Japanese were finding it harder every day to supply their beachhead from Rabaul. 'Secret transport', as they called it, was essential to escape the Allied planes that had caused the Navy to refuse Adachi any more destroyers. Submarines were the best recourse, but they were few. The only hope was to use landing barges that could move at night, hiding out in sheltered coves by day. The barges were plentiful enough but the men to operate them were not, because General Imamura had turned over the main strength of 18th Army's shipping engineer unit to 17th Army for use at Guadalcanal – his first priority.

Before leaving Tokyo for Rabaul in late November, Imamura had gone to the Imperial Palace to receive his orders. As he was bowing himself out, the Emperor called out, 'Imamura! I understand that my soldiers are suffering terribly in Guadalcanal. Go as soon as you can and save them. Even one day is important.' Tears glistened on his cheeks.

Imamura considered that he had made a personal vow to

the Emperor. Though General Hyakutake warned him from the Solomons that his position was desperate, troops living on grass roots and water, a hundred starving to death every day, Imamura sent a message to the men on Guadalcanal asking them to 'set His Majesty's heart at ease' by retaking the island.

In tokyo the Army General Staff was determined to win a victory in Guadalcanal, demanding men and supplies and ships to transport them. The demands for additional shipping, in the face of constant attrition from U.S. Navy and Air Force attacks, began to be more and more firmly opposed by the War Ministry, backed by the Japanese Navy. Violent arguments erupted, on one occasion leading to a fist fight.

As December wore on, with Hyakutake pathetically appealing for permission to break into the enemy's positions and die an honorable death rather than die of hunger in our own foxholes,' the Army General Staff could not help realizing that withdrawal was the only course. But it seemed incapable of admitting it. At a meeting on Christmas Day between Army and Navy leaders at the Imperial Palace, the debate broke out all over again.

One Army hothead bitterly accused the Navy, 'You landed the Army without arms and food and then cut off the supply. It's like sending someone on a roof and taking away the ladder.'

In New Guinea also, the ladder had been taken away. To carry supplies to the beachhead and evacuate the wounded, General Adachi had only his landing barges; crews would have to be trained to operate them. He selected likely young engineers and gave them a week's training in handling engines and navigating the big clumsy boats.

The barge project came too late to help the garrison at Buna Station. On December 26 Adachi ordered General Yamagata, whose headquarters was still north of Gona, to move all his troops by sea to Sanananda and from there attempt a rescue of the Buna garrison; if he failed, he was to hold at Sanananda. While Yamagata was getting his men forward, moving at night by barge, Adachi came to the conclusion that the rescue attempt was hopeless. He ordered Buna Government Station to be evacuated on December 28, its defenders to try to make their way to Sanananda.

General Eichelberger, unaware that the battle for Buna Station had already been won, was in the last days of December making ever more frantic efforts to 'push on to victory'.

Strenuous efforts were made to take advantage of the one breakthrough on Christmas Day, when a company had reached the coastal area. On the following day a platoon under Major Edmund R. Schroeder managed to get through to the isolated position, just before dark. Schroeder found the men in misery, huddled in a swamp. Unable to bury their dead or care for their wounded, and badly shaken by constant Japanese attacks, the men were completely demoralized. He set to work to restore them as a fighting unit. He got the dead buried and the wounded treated and reorganized the troops, placing them in the best possible position for defense, awaiting reinforcements.

But could reinforcements get through? Attempts were made on the morning of December 27 but failed. During the morning Zeros bombed the Urbana front and in the afternoon the Japanese set a fire in Government Gardens. A great grass fire swept the whole front.

Late that night the 32d Division's Chief of Staff, Colonel J. Sladen Bradley, who had been at the front all day, came back to Eichelberger's headquarters with an alarming report. His briefing in the general's tent at two o'clock in the morning indicated that the troops on the Urbana front were suffering from battle shock and had become incapable of advancing. A number of Eichelberger's senior officers were convinced that the situation was desperate.

When the conference was over Eichelberger lay down and tried to sleep, but sleep would not come. A deep depression settled upon him. He remembered General MacArthur striding up and down the veranda at Government House ordering him to take Buna, and later turning to him and repeating his bitter question, 'Must I always lead a forlorn hope?' Tossing on his cot in the steaming tropical night, Eichelberger could imagine General MacArthur's consternation at the bad news from the front that day.

Next morning things looked brighter. 'Daylight,' observed Eichelberger, 'is good medicine for the fears of darkness.' Even better medicine was the arrival during the morning of General Sutherland with good news. Reinforcements were on the way. The 163d Regiment of the 41st Division, a well-trained unit under a respected officer, Colonel Jens A. Doe, had reached Port Moresby from Australia. General Herring asked for it; but General MacArthur sent word to Blamey by Sutherland that it was to go to the Urbana front.

Eichelberger took Sutherland forward to Colonel Grose's command post. Arriving shortly after noon, they learned that fresh companies of the 127th Regiment had managed to break through to Schroeder's force; ammunition and food were getting through, the wounded had been evacuated, and the troops were being organized for action.

Encouraged by this success, Grose had just ordered the 127th's depleted and exhausted 3d Battalion, which had been attacking at Government Gardens, taken out of the line for a rest.

The briefings at Grose's command post had hardly been concluded when Eichelberger, suddenly and without any warning to Grose, ordered an immediate, two-pronged, attack on Buna Station, to take place that very afternoon. The 3d Battalion, called back into action, was to attack on the left over the Japanese footbridge on Musita Island, while Schroeder's men pushed forward from the right.

Startled by the abrupt order, Grose concluded that Eichelberger was trying to impress Sutherland. And indeed the temptation must have been irresistible – to take Buna in the presence of MacArthur's 'eyes and ears'!

With deep misgivings, Grose hurriedly arranged for a late afternoon attack. The hardest problem was the Japanese footbridge, which had a 15-foot gap on the far end, made by a recent Allied artillery hit. To allow time for the bridge to be repaired, so that the main body of troops could cross on it, forty men in five assault boats were to paddle around the island, land east of the bridge, and engage the Japanese.

In the slanting sunshine of late afternoon the boats from their hiding place, under the jungle growth on the southern bank of the island, began to push off as the first artillery salvo boomed out. But they went in the wrong direction, west instead of east; and tried to land on the western of the two sand spits north of the island, the one known as the 'village spit' because it ran east from Buna Village. There the defenders of the village spit mistook them for the enemy and fired upon them. Miraculously no one was killed, but all the boats were sunk.

In the meantime, six men who had volunteered to repair the bridge ran out on it carrying three heavy planks; dropping them in place, one man was killed. Then troops of the 3d Battalion began to run across, but when those in the lead reached the newly laid planks the pilings collapsed and the men were thrown into the water.

The attack had been an utter failure. Eichelberger, much wrought up, 'ranted and raved,' Grose observed, 'like a caged lion.' He knew what Sutherland's report to MacArthur would be. Later, Sutherland told Grose that when he reported the 'fiasco' to MacArthur, Eichelberger was 'never closer to being relieved.'

But once again – in the harrowing ups and downs of the general's efforts to 'push on to victory' – on the heels of the fiasco came good news. At dusk on December 28 a patrol cautiously probing the Triangle discovered that the Japanese had gone, evidently in a hurry, leaving quantities of ammunition in the bunkers and fire trenches. Though the Triangle had apparently been evacuated on orders, Eichelberger inferred that his advance into Government Gardens had made it untenable; he was soon in fact boasting that the 'famous "Triangle" which held us up so long, was finally taken.'

Encouraging reports came also from the Warren front. By December 28 Wootten's Americans and Australians had overrun the antiaircraft guns that had mowed down the tanks on Old Strip and had achieved a line less than half a mile south of Giropa Point – the last enemy stronghold on the Warren front. Though the Japanese were putting up a sporadic but fierce delaying fight, becoming 'savagely alive' along Old Strip on December 29, Wootten was confident that he could take Giropa Point in a few days, as soon as he received a fresh battalion of his 18th Brigade, commanded by Lieutenant Colonel A. S. W. Arnold. On New Year's Day, Arnold was to lead an all-out attack on Giropa Point.

Eichelberger was eagerly awaiting his own reinforcements, the 163d Infantry of the 41st Division; and on the morning of December 30, as he was sitting in his tent talking with Colonel Lief J. Sverdrup, an Engineer visitor from Port Moresby, he was gratified by the arrival of Colonel Doe, the 163d's commander, accompanied by Generals Herring and Vasey.

While tea was being prepared, Eichelberger, turning to Doe,

proposed a visit to the front so that Doe could see where the 163d was to go. All at once, silence fell in the tent. Doe seemed to be waiting for the Australian generals to say something. When they remained silent, he said he had been informed that the 163d was to go to the Sanananda front. Eichelberger was dumbfounded. Obviously MacArthur had reversed his decision to give him the regiment. The reason (he learned later) was a vigorous protest from Blamey.

General Herring rubbed salt in the wound by suggesting that Eichelberger 'take it easy' for the next two days, since Wootten was not going to do anything that day or the next. He even intimated that perhaps Buna Station had been abandoned.

The Australian generals had their tea and departed, taking Doe with them. Sverdrup, Eichelberger reported to Sutherland, 'gained the same impression you have gained' that the Australians were 'not anxious' for the Americans to capture Buna Station before they had reached Giropa Point.

Eichelberger had been intending 'sure as hell' to rest his own troops the following day. He changed his mind. He decided to throw everything he had into a major attack on December 31, a day ahead of the Australians' offensive on Giropa.

The attack was to be launched by the two companies who were already on the village spit north of Musita Island. They were to cross to the spit extending west from Buna Station (no Japanese were there) around four in the morning when the tide was out and the shallows between the two spits were no more than ankle deep. While this movement was under way, aided by companies on Musita Island using the Japanese footbridge, Schroeder's force was to attack Buna on the right flank and a third force was to advance in the center from Government Gardens.

At 4.30 on the morning of December 31, while it was still dark, the troops began to splash single file through the shallows between the two spits. Because surprise was of the greatest importance, they had been ordered to advance silently and on no account to fire weapons until ordered to do so. But when the lead column had gone several yards up the Buna Station spit, the men saw two Japanese landing barges stranded on the beach and could not resist the temptation to throw grenades into them. Immediately, green and red Japanese flares lit up the whole area and heavy fire poured down upon the spit. The Americans panicked and began running toward the rear.

Colonel Grose, standing on the village spit, stationed himself in their path, pistol in hand. He stopped a lieutenant leading the retreat and ordered him to return. The young officer refused. Grose sent him to the rear under arrest and ordered a sergeant to take the retreating company back up the Buna Station spit. He did so, and the men dug in, alongside the follow-up company, in water-filled foxholes. There the whole force was to remain for the next three days.

Eichelberger's troops on the right and center made little progress on December 31. His gamble had failed, so disastrously that he was unable to mount a strong Urbana front attack on New Year's Day. The best he could promise General Sutherland was that he would push one of Major Schroeder's companies eastward toward Giropa Point to help the attack on the Warren front.

The main effort in clearing the Japanese from the Buna area was to be made by Brigadier Wootten.

New Year's Day dawned clear and fine for Wootten's attack on Giropa Point. A light breeze from the sea blew cool and refreshing on the faces of Lieutenant Colonel Arnold's Australians as they waited in the kunai grass facing the coconut plantation barring the way to the beach. Ahead of them were six tanks; behind them were three supporting battalions, one Australian and two American.

At first light the artillery opened up and at eight o'clock the tanks moved out. When they reached the coconut plantation, Arnold's infantrymen ran up to close in on their flanks and rear, followed by an American battalion commanded by Lieutenant Colonel Alexander J. MacNab.

'Everybody's spirits were high,' MacNab later remembered; with 'much comradely rivalry and friendly recrimination' he and Arnold led their men into the fight 'with a sort of old-time flourish'.

The infantrymen – at last – had a weapon that would defeat the bunkers. Made by Australian engineers, it was a bomb screwed into a can of explosive. After a tank had scattered the Japanese protecting the bunker on the outside, it would bear down on the bunker and knock off a corner; an infantryman would creep up, toss in the bomb, and duck. The explosion would rock the bunker, and stupefy the Japanese inside. Then the bunker could be burned out by throwing in a can of gasoline ignited by tracers.

Subduing the strongpoints with the aid of the tanks, in less than an hour the Australians reached the beach and made known their success by shooting a signal into the sky. As they closed in on the main Japanese position at Giropa, the resistance stiffened; two Australian company commanders were killed and one company was cut to pieces. But by dark the last pocket of enemy resistance was destroyed. Night brought thunder, lightning, and rain. In the lightning flashes, Japanese soldiers were seen out in the sea swimming westward from Giropa Point and from Buna Station as well.

At daylight on January 2, 1943, Americans on the Urbana front from their foxholes in the sandy spit west of Buna Station saw that the waters offshore were swarming with Japanese, some in small boats, others swimming or clinging to boxes, rafts, and logs.

That morning, artillery pounded and rocked Buna Government Station. White phosphorus shells set fire to grass, trees, and wooden buildings. But the Japanese were still full of fight. When the American troops moved forward from the spit, the swamp, and Schroeder's coastal enclave on the east, Japanese fire erupted from bunkers and from snipers in the trees; a sniper's bullet crashed into the skull of Major Schroeder, who fell mortally wounded. Not until midafternoon were the troops able to break into the compound that had once been Buna Government Station.

They beheld a scene of death and devastation – Japanese bodies everywhere; charred, smoking, buildings and topless trees; the ground pitted with shell holes. Beyond, the beach was strewn with abandoned weapons and wrecked landing barges.

While the Americans were overrunning Buna Station on January 2, Arnold with four tanks was cruising his battlefield, mopping up isolated bunkers.

That day, the two Japanese commanders, Colonel Yamamoto and Captain Yasuda, who had hastened eastward from Buna Station to join Yamamoto, both 'died facing the enemy tanks', according to a Japanese account. As Arnold's tanks approached the bunker that had been Yamamoto's command post, two Japanese officers emerged from the bunker. Arnold called out to them to surrender. They gave no sign that they heard him. He repeated his call and was again ignored.

One of the officers slowly moved out of sight. The other washed himself in the brackish water of Simemi Creek and drank some of it. Still disregarding the men silently watching him, he bowed very low three times into the morning sun. Then he turned and stood erect, facing the Australians.

Arnold called out: 'I'll give you until I count ten to surrender!'

Without a word the officer took out a small Japanese flag and tied one end to his sword. Raising the sword in his right hand, he held the other end of the flag in his left, so that the flag covered his breast. Arnold counted slowly. When he came to 'Nine,' the Japanese officer shouted 'Out!' The Australians riddled him. The other officer was found dead, hanging from a tree.

The Australians took only one prisoner that day; the day before they took only eight, and six of them were Chinese coolies. Everywhere the Japanese had fought bravely to the death for their Emperor. Eventually 1,400 were buried at Buna, 900 each of Giropa Point and 500 west of it.

On the Allied side, the Urbana and Warren Forces had lost 620 men killed – 353 Americans and 267 Australians; 2,065 wounded, 132 missing.

On Sunday, January 3, the front from Buna Village to Cape Endaiadere was 'almost peaceful', observed Tillman Durdin of the New York *Times*. Rain fell off and on all day. Walking along the coast, Durdin heard a shot now and then and an occasional burst of mortar fire, but for the most part the front was a scene of 'quiet desolation', the only sound the rain drumming on the shattered palms.

Some of the American troops went swimming in the sea, some washed out their fatigues (for the first time in weeks), some 'simply slept the deep, deep sleep of exhaustion, curled up under the shell-shattered palms or in sandy foxholes.' Durdin noted that their faces were gaunt and haggard, many flushed with fever; and that the knees and elbows poking through ragged uniforms were pathetically bony.

To the rain-drenched tents of commanders there were delivered messages of congratulation from Generals Blamey and Herring. From General MacArthur no message came.

Eichelberger, ascribing MacArthur's silence to the circumstance that bad weather had grounded some of the flights from Port Moresby, was busy the following day, January 4, conferring with the Australians on plans for the capture of Sanananda. They did not know the enemy's strength there, whether they would face a thousand Japanese or five thousand. In any case they planned to launch an attack as soon as the rest of Doe's 163d Infantry arrived and Wootten's 18th Brigade could be brought from Giropa.

On January 5, the weather cleared and planeloads of high-ranking officers flew in from Port Moresby, among them General Blamey, who insisted on touring the whole front in a jeep. The most important American officer arriving that day was Major General Horace H. Fuller, commanding general of the 41st Division, who was to be responsible for the defense of the Buna coast at the end of the campaign.

The planes brought no message from General MacArthur. Eichelberger, writing to General Sutherland that he had not heard from 'any of you good people,' plaintively asked, 'Is your secretary sick?'

On January 9 came the first word from General MacArthur.

January 8, 1943

Dear Bob:
I am returning to G.H.Q., Brisbane, Saturday morning the 9th, so will not see you until some later time. I have been wanting to personally congratulate you on the success that has been achieved. As soon as Fuller takes hold, I want you to return to the mainland. There are many important things with reference to rehabilitation and training that will necessitate your immediate effort. The 32nd Division should be evacuated as soon as possible so that it can be rejuvenated.
I am so glad that you were not injured in the fighting.
I always feared that your incessant exposure might result fatally.
With a hearty slap on the back,

Most cordially,
MacArthur.

The day this note was written, MacArthur's communiqué stated that the campaign in New Guinea was 'in its final closing phase', since the Sanananda position had been 'completely enveloped'; and asserted that the annihilation of the Japanese army had been accomplished. His Order of the Day on January 9, issued after his return to Brisbane, awarded twelve Distinguished Service Crosses to an assortment of Allied generals and brigadiers, praised the troops for defeating 'a bold and aggressive enemy'; and thanked God for granting 'success in our great Crusade'.

The triumphant press releases emanating from General MacArthur's headquarters were read with foreboding by the Australian commanders on the Sanananda front. They knew they were facing a savage enemy who would fight to the death, as at Buna, and that victory would not be easy. General Eichelberger was sure that many of the Australian commanders foresaw 'the ruin of their own careers – and mine.'

CHAPTER XIV

THE END AT SANANANDA

Early on Christmas morning a party of Australian soldiers carrying wounded men on stretchers made their way down a jungle trail skirting the Sanananda Road. It was a bright, sunny day, already hot. The soldiers moved slowly under their heavy burdens, four men to a stretcher, and walked warily, each carrying his rifle in his free hand, because the trail wound through a maze of Japanese bunkers. These seemed to have been abandoned, but the soldiers could never be sure.

As the party neared Huggins Roadblock the going became easier. Then the men came to a clearing where they beheld a scene so macabre that they stopped in horror. The rays of the sun, penetrating tangled vines hanging from the trees, shone on skeletons peering from the windows of roofless huts and illuminated the bones of horses draped with rotting saddles.

This was the Japanese camp the Americans had shot up when they broke through to establish Huggins Roadblock nearly a month before.

A second roadblock, 400 yards up the road, had just been achieved by Australian troops newly arrived at the front. They called it Kano. It was from Kano that the stretcher party was carrying the wounded, using the jungle trail because the Sanananda Road between the two roadblocks was still under Japanese fire.

The fresh Australian troops had been flown over the mountains in mid-December. They were the last reinforcements Port Moresby could furnish. From Gona – the only other source of reinforcements – General Vasey had just brought to Sanananda Honner's 39th Battalion, without, however, Lieutenant Colonel Honner, who was down with malaria. The battalion was in bad shape. When it returned to Gona from Haddy's Village, many of the men could hardly walk; with feet 'red-raw and white-swollen', they 'hobbled weakly about in bandages instead of boots'. After only one day of rest they were sent to Sanananda.

When the 39th Battalion hobbled into Huggins Roadblock on the afternoon of December 22, the badly battered company of American infantrymen limped out. Painfully the Americans made their way south to join the remnants of other companies of the 126th Infantry who were positioned with two Australian battalions facing strong Japanese defenses at the Track Junction. From there two tracks led to the coast, one left to Cape Killerton (east of Gona), the other right to Sanananda. Determined to hold at this vital point, the Japanese were nightly erupting from their bunkers in violent counterattacks.

Wounds as well as sickness and exhaustion continued to take a heavy toll of the Americans of the 126th, who had been on the Sanananda front longer than anyone still there; and not until January 9 were they permitted to leave. On that day, of the 1,400 infantrymen of the 126th who had gone into action the third week of November, less than two hundred effectives were left.

Marching off to Buna, they were welcomed there by General Eichelberger with band music and a martial ceremony. 'Actually it was a melancholy homecoming,' he remembered later. The men who answered the muster 'were so ragged and so pitiful that when I greeted them my eyes were wet.'

General Herring's plans for the capture of Sanananda made it plain that the battle was to be an Australian show. The only American force under American command was Colonel Grose's 127th Infantry, which was to advance on Sanananda along the coastal track leading westward from Buna Village; and Grose could do little more than block the Japanese on the narrow coastal track, in places under water at high tide, the ocean waves washing over it and spilling into a deep swamp on the other side. Colonel Doe's 163d Infantry was under Australian command. By the second week in January, Doe had relieved the Australians at the Huggins and Kano Roadblocks and had a force astride the track to Cape Killerton. His role in the battle was to block road and track in support of an advance on the Track Junction by Brigadier Wootten's 18th Brigade.

Wootten was to make the main attack. He had been reinforced with about a thousand men – but he was short on tanks. He had been able to bring only four with him from the Buna front before heavy rains, washing out bridges and softening the ground, made further movement impossible. He planned to use three of them (keeping one in reserve) to spearhead a thrust by Lieutenant Colonel Arnold's battalion into the Track Junction, using the log-corduroyed Sanananda Road, the only footing that would support tanks.

The attack began at eight o'clock on the morning of January 12.

The morning mists were just lifting when the lead tank lurched up the Sanananda Road. After 60 yards, just as its commander halted it, looking for a bunker, a Japanese antitank gun struck, its shells smashing through the tank and bursting inside. When the second tank came up, it was hit by a fusilade that mortally wounded its commander. The third tank was completely destroyed; bursting into flames, probably from a mine, it was gutted and all the crew perished.

The infantry companies in the attack fared little better. Caught as if by barbed wire in the tangled branches of trees torn and twisted by artillery fire, the infantrymen were picked off by the Japanese and forced back, time after time. By the end of the day, Arnold's battalion had scarcely advanced and had lost four officers and ninety-five men. A supporting battalion was stopped by punishing fire that killed the commanders of the two lead companies; its casualties were six officers and twenty-seven men.

General Vasey was deeply discouraged by the failure of the attack. It seemed to him that even if more tanks could be brought up, they would be knocked out, and that without tanks the infantrymen could not defeat the bunkers.

For advice he turned to General Eichelberger, who had just taken over the command of Advanced New Guinea Force. The following day Eichelberger arrived on the Sanananda front and after a conference with the Australian commanders, he decided against any further attacks on the Track Junction. All the conferees agreed that the best plan was to surround it and cut off supplies. The Track Junction was the Triangle on the Urbana front all over again, an isolated position so strongly held that it could not be stormed without losses too great to be borne.

Next day the resemblance to the Triangle became even more marked. Early on January 14 one of Colonel Doe's patrols came upon a sick Japanese lying in some bushes. He said his colonel had received orders the night before to evacuate the Track Junction. By early afternoon Wootten's men had swept through the abandoned position, discovering only six living men in a welter of 152 bodies. They found the gun that had demolished the tanks, also a quantity of machine guns and rifles, about a third of them Australian.

That night reports came to General Herring indicating a Japanese withdrawal from the coast west of Gona. Patrols met no Japanese and learned from natives that landing barges filled with Japanese soldiers had been seen leaving the mouth of the Kumusi River.

On the last day of December the Emperor of Japan, 'anxious about the state of the fighting at Guadalcanal and Buna', summoned the Chiefs of Staff of his Navy and Army and commanded them to make a study of the situation on both fronts. After reading the study, he came to the conclusion that both Guadalcanal and Buna should be abandoned. Thereupon, on January 4, Imperial General Headquarters issued orders to General Imamura at Rabaul to withdraw the Buna force up the coast of New Guinea to Lae and Salamaua, the Guadalcanal force to be evacuated to the northern Solomons.

Imamura was unwilling to transmit the order to Sanananda by wireless because he feared the message would be intercepted; consequently he appointed a special messenger, Major Hakatsuki, to carry the plan of retreat to General Oda. The major left Rabaul by submarine and was never heard from again. The submarine was evidently lost at sea, probably destroyed by Allied aircraft when it surfaced in the dangerous waters of Dampier Strait.

With no way of knowing that the withdrawal had been ordered, Oda pleaded with Rabaul for supplies and reinforcements. On his arrival at Sanananda late in December he had promised the troops that the Emperor would never give up the position, and had even aroused hopes of eventually attacking Port Moresby. Morale rose.

Buoyed by hope, Sergeant Kiyoshi Wada, a medical corpsman attached to the hospital at Giruwa, a native village marking the eastern perimeter of the Sanananda base, wrote in his diary on December 22: *To have spent over five months on this island of distress and sorrow, enduring starvation and hardships and carrying on a battle, is good training which comes but once in a lifetime for a man.*

Wada had recurring malaria and he was hungry all the time. Some days a little rice or a handful of dried vegetables came in, but sometimes no rations came. Around Christmas he was tantalized by reports that front-line soldiers had found Christmas packages – containing sweets! – on the bodies of Australian soldiers. His Christmas Eve supper was coconut and octopus, on Christmas Day, a handful of rice. Once he caught a few crabs in the ocean and ate them raw; once he ate snakes. As the days went by, he and his comrades were reduced to eating grass. *We are just like horses.* By January 10 *all the grass and roots have been eaten in the Giruwa area.* That night heavy rains came, flooding the hospital wards. Next day the enemy shelling increased. Wada wrote in his diary: *I am troubled. I am troubled.*

On January 12 General Oda sent an urgent radio to Rabaul. His men were starving. Most had dysentery. Those not ill in bed were too weak for hand-to-hand fighting. If reinforcements were not landed at once, 'We are doomed.'

Adachi sent by radio on January 13 the lost plan for evacuating Sanananda. The troops were to withdraw westward to the mouths of the Kumusi and Mambare rivers by landing barge, on foot, or by swimming; from there they would march or be taken by sea to Lae and Salamaua. The sick and wounded were to be evacuated by landing barge immediately. The movement of the able-bodied was to begin after dark. On January 25, when the moon was favorable.

If Adachi's radio ordering the withdrawal had been intercepted by Allied Intelligence (it was not); or if, lacking definite intelligence, Allied commanders had correctly estimated their success in cutting off Oda's supplies and correctly interpreted reports of Japanese withdrawals up the coast toward Lae, the Japanese at Sanananda might have been merely contained and left to starve, and many lives would have been saved. But in the third week of January the Australians were still attacking, determined (as Eichelberger had been at Buna Station) to 'push on to Victory'.

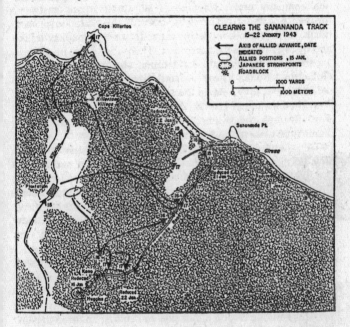

The final push began on the morning of January 15.

General Vasey had ordered Brigadier Wootten to seize the Cape Killerton area, then move eastward down the coast on Sanananda, while Colonel Doe overcame the strongpoint facing him and moving up the Sanananda Road.

Early in the morning Wootten sent three battalions (keeping one battalion in reserve) up the Cape Killerton track, which swung northwest from the Track Junction and wound through a narrow strip of kunai grass bordered by swampland. The track was dry (the sun had been shining for two days) and the men made good time to a coconut plantation several miles up the track.

From there one battalion was sent ahead to reconnoiter the approaches to Cape Killerton. These men had not gone very far before they made a dismaying discovery. The Killerton track disappeared into a mangrove swamp. All afternoon they searched for it and at night lay down to sleep in water or 'perched in trees like wet fowls'. Next morning, in desperation, one company under Captain F. W. Cook struck eastward through the swamp. The main body of the battalion pushed north, up to their armpits in water, found a secondary track, and by nightfall reached the coast. There they came up against Japanese pillboxes of the kind found also on the beaches at Gona and Buna. These coastal defenses were so strongly defended that they held up the Australian battalion for days.

In the meantime, Captain Cook's company, wallowing eastward through the swamp, found itself in late afternoon on January 16 close to the Sanananda Road.

This changed the direction of the attack. Wootten decided to strike directly at the Sanananda Road through the swamp. At last light on January 16 the movement began, led by Lieutenant Colonel Arnold. During the night a violent thunderstorm broke. Lightning struck into the swamp water, shocking some of the men struggling through it. Thunder rolled up and down the coast; heavy rain came down hard.

This was the curtain raiser to the last act at Sanananda. Drenching rains swelled the swamps, so that in the mud and water every movement was slow motion, as in a nightmare. By noon on January 17 when the first of Arnold's men reached the Sanananda Road they found it looking like a causeway, with torrents running fast on either side and boiling up through gaps in the road made by Allied bombs.

By nightfall Arnold was holding about 300 yards of the road in a perilous perimeter. Just ahead was a Japanese stronghold barring the way to Sanananda. Behind him was a big pocket that Colonel Doe had been unable to overcome, containing the main Japanese headquarters in the area, presumably that of Colonel Yokoyama. It was to hold out until the end; not until January 22 was Doe able to overcome it.

Blocked on the Sanananda Road, Wootten again changed the direction of his attack. He sent his reserve battalion across the swamp directly to Sanananda Point, bypassing the road. He believed that the Japanese were counting on the swamp to protect them, and he was right. Encountering little resistance, the Australians entered Sanananda Point on the morning of January 18. They found a scene of watery desolation: a demolished warehouse, the roof of what had once been an Australian rest house, ruins of a 'boy house' (for native workers) lying in the slime, wrecked barges on the beach, and everywhere mud, water-filled bomb craters, and dripping splintered palm trees. The Japanese had evidently pulled back all troops to Giruwa, about half a mile to the east.

Though the enemy held out for several days at their strongpoints on the Sanananda Road, exacting a heavy toll in Australian and American casualties, the curtain was soon to be rung down on this scene of 'mud, filth and death'.

On January 19, General Yamagata as senior Japanese commander ordered the withdrawal of the 18th Army at dark on January 20, instead of January 25. After sending his orders to General Oda at Giruwa and Colonel Yazawa, who was blocking Grose's Americans east of Giruwa, Yamagata departed by landing barge for the Kumusi River.

The withdrawal of the sick and wounded by landing barge was already well under way, made possible by the arrival in New Guinea of the fleet of barges manned by newly trained engineers. Successfully navigating the dangerous Dampier Strait in the darkness of night without even a compass to guide them, they escaped Allied planes and submarines and after 450 hazardous sea miles made port at Mambare. From there they proceeded cautiously down the coast to the Sanananda area, moving only at night and hiding out by day.

Their coming was awaited with great anxiety. When they pulled into the lagoon at Giruwa, the sick and wounded crawled toward them or were carried on the shoulders of those able to walk. Watching the boats pull out one evening in heavy rain, Sergeant Wada stood on the beach in misery. Some of the hospital attendants had been put aboard to care for the patients, but he had been left behind. He remembered how when he came to New Guinea he had been willing to die at any time. But now, wasted by malaria and starvation, he longed with all his heart to go home. Praying that his commanding officer would not leave him behind, he returned to the hospital and was killed by shellfire.

General Oda, having completed the arrangements for the retreat with the help of his supply officer, Lieutenant Colonel Yoshinobu Tomita, saw that they were carried out on the night of January 20.

Among the men slipping away westward into the swamps was Colonel Yazawa, who had arrived in New Guinea with General Horii in August and fought valiantly and well for his Emperor in the mountains and on the Buna coast. Yazawa, who had engineered the brilliant withdrawal from Oivi, was not to survive the retreat from Sanananda. He was killed when he ran into an Australian outpost.

When the last unit had disappeared into the darkness, General Oda said to the soldier on duty, 'That's the end of that. I am going to smoke one cigarette at leisure.'

Then as the man hesitated, the general ordered, 'March on.'

The soldier went off to catch up with the last unit, but had not gone far when he heard pistol shots in the rear. Hurrying back to see whether the enemy had started a fight, he found the bodies of General Oda and Lieutenant Colonel Tomita lying on a cloak on the ground where they had shot themselves.

The last battle on the Sanananda Road was fought by Colonel Doe. In the darkness before dawn on January 22, Doe's men were awakened by the rustle of movements through the swamps around them. The Japanese were trying to escape to the west. Thirty-three were killed. In midmorning Doe advanced against the last remaining strongpoint. Going in on the run behind the final mortar salvo, the attackers quickly overcame the strongpoint. The rest of the day, in all the positions along the Sanananda Road, Doe's men hunted out and destroyed the last-ditch fighters in their water-filled foxholes and bunkers.

The heavy rains of the past week stopped. The skies cleared; and as the sound of firing died away at Sanananda in the dying day, a glorious tropical sunset flung banners of rose and gold across the western sky.

CHAPTER XV

'NO MORE BUNAS'

'A striking victory' at Buna was proclaimed in an Allied communiqué on January 22, 1943. The enemy had been 'annihilated'.

For the first time in World War II, the Japanese Army had been decisively defeated. Guadalcanal was not declared. won until February 9.

Of these two earliest campaigns in the Pacific, each lasting six months almost to the day, Buna had been the bloodier. At Guadalcanal, of some 60,000 Americans committed, about 1,600 were killed and 4,245 were wounded. At Buna, of a total of about 40,000 Australians and Americans, 3,095 were killed and 5,451 were wounded, not counting losses from illness. Most of the troops had at one time or another suffered from malaria, dysentery, or dengue fever; more than two hundred had succumbed to the deadly scrub typhus.

Battalions had been cut down to company size or less. Lieutenant Colonel Honner's Australian 39th Battalion, marching to Dobodura airfield for the flight home on January 24, could muster only seven officers and twenty-five men – 'haggard, silent, sweating scarecrows under the tropic sun'. The battalion of the American 126th Regiment on the Sanananda front had lost all but six officers and ninety-two men; the regiment's 'Ghost Mountain' battalion was down to six officers and 126 men.

Twenty years later, an American officer who fought with the 32d Division in its two-year advance from New Guinea to the northern Philippines looked back in horror on Buna as his worst experience of the war.

'The toughest fighting in the world,' was the judgment of an Australian historian, George H. Johnston. American historian Samuel Eliot Morison would not agree that Buna was tougher than Italy, Tarawa, Iwo Jima, Okinawa, Peleliu or Guadalcanal but conceded that the fighting was 'certainly the nastiest' of the war.

The battleground had been a vast, primitive, almost unknown wilderness of towering mountains and steaming coastal jungles, burned by the equatorial sun and drenched by tropical downpours. Into this fearsome terrain had been thrown raw Australian militiamen and American National Guardsmen, none of them adequately trained for combat of any kind. The Australian regulars who reinforced these men were veterans, but their battles had been fought not in the jungle but in the deserts of Egypt and the mountains of Greece.

Few of the Allied troops had had any training in what the Australians called 'bushcraft' – the art of surviving in the jungle; or had been given the gear that might have made life in New Guinea bearable. The khaki shorts of the Australians exposed their legs to insect bites; the trousers of the Americans, thick with dye, caused jungle ulcers. Simple ordinary items such as machetes for cutting through undergrowth had not been issued, or insect repellents, or waterproof pouches that would have kept salt tablets and quinine from disintegrating in the rain, and cigarettes and matches from becoming sodden. The diet (repugnant to the Americans) was the traditional Australian Army ration of corned beef, rice, and tea. Special rations for tropical warfare would have helped.

'Lack of planning, lack of appreciation of the Japanese' characterized the New Guinea campaign from the beginning, according to Osmar White, who was there. The enemy had been well prepared. The Japanese planners had actually gone into the jungle and learned what was necessary for survival. They gave the Japanese soldier a cloth to wear under his helmet to keep sweat from running into his eyes and provided him with salt plums to add to his rice. They trained him thoroughly in outflanking tactics and supplied him with light, efficient weapons, such as the gun that could be manhandled over the mountains. The Allies had lacked effective weapons and means of getting them to the front. On the Kokoda Track they did not have guns with enough range to stop the Japanese; on the coast they had no way to overcome the Japanese bunkers. They did not have landing craft that would have enabled them to launch a seaborne invasion of Buna. Buna had been (in General Eichelberger's words) 'a poor man's war', fought at a time when the eyes of planners in the United States were fixed on other theaters. Such landing craft as could be spared for the Pacific went to Guadalcanal. Also, tank-mounted flame-throwers that would later defeat Japanese bunkers had not yet been developed.

To supply such needs there was little General MacArthur could do. Yet he might have pressed harder for tanks and heavy artillery, which would have been helpful in the early days of the campaign. That he did not do so was presumably because he relied too heavily on the advice of his Air officer, General Kenney: it had yet to be demonstrated that in jungle warfare bombers cannot live up to the claims of Air officers.

To a remarkable degree, MacArthur was swayed by staff officers he trusted. Relying completely on General Sutherland, his 'eyes and ears', he never went nearer the front than his hasty visit to the beginning of the Kokoda Track in early October. His decision to remain in the rear was, in the opinion of General Brett, a throwback to World War I – 'a repetition of Pershin's attitude'. In World War I, MacArthur had been a courageous front-line officer; but he had then been a divisional commander, a different category from Supreme Commander.

His conviction that the place of the Supreme Commander was in the rear was probably reinforced by his own inclinations. He was essentially a private person, not outgoing. On his arrival in Melbourne, when the Australians were eager to honor him, he refused all invitations; there and later at Brisbane he spent his evenings with his wife and child at his hotel. At Port Moresby in the darkest days of the campaign he remained at Government House, his 'Ivory Tower'. In Brett's words, he 'had little to do with soldiers'.

MacArthur's ignorance of the terrain in New Guinea cost many lives, as the men who had been forced to cross 'Ghost Mountain' could testify. His ignorance of conditions at the front led him throughout the campaign to make impossible demands on his front-line commanders to 'drive through to objectives regardless of losses' and 'take Buna today at all costs'.

In issuing such orders, MacArthur seemed to Australian historian John Vader (who was in New Guinea at the time) 'to have developed the mantle of the mad imperious general of the First War', believing 'that all commanders should drive their troops non-stop at the enemy, a continuous never-ending charge regardless of casualties.' Such generals, Vader comments, 'would have made excellent Japanese privates'.

The determination of the Japanese private to fight to the death for his Emperor was noted time after time in New Guinea. He would fight on, even after he knew his cause was hopeless: horrible evidence of this was discovered in the bunkers at Gona in December.

Between July and December of 1942 the Japanese put ashore on the Buna coast about 18,000 men, of which some 15,000 were front-line soldiers or marines. After the withdrawal from the Owen Stanley Range, fighting strength was down to 11,880 men. Between November 19 and January 22, total casualties were 8,000. Of the Japanese soldiers remaining after January 22, many were cut down by Allied fire as they retreated, or died of disease. When the remnants were assembled at Lae in March of 1943, General Adachi flew from Rabaul to inspect them. He saw that they were no longer fit for duty and sent them back to Japan.

'A magnificent tragedy,' the Japanese termed their New Guinea campaign.

The officers who planned it had been, like MacArthur, ignorant of the terrain; they had underestimated the risks involved in crossing the Owen Stanley Range. Their intelligence, like his, had been faulty. MacArthur was surprised by the landing at Buna; the Japanese were thrown off-balance by the American landing at Guadalcanal.

Japanese war correspondent Seizo Okada on his return to Rabaul from New Guinea in late November found the town 'buzzing with the staff officers dispatched from the Imperial Headquarters in Tokyo'. All were preoccupied with Guadalcanal. When he mentioned New Guinea 'they turned away with an air of being bored'.

Early in December Okada attended a press conference held

by Colonel Masanobu Tsuji, a staff officer who was on his way back to Tokyo after a month on Guadalcanal. Tsuji, a man with a round face, bald head, and small blinking eyes, was extremely influential; younger staff officers 'revered him as Japan's "God of Operations".' He was full of admiration for the way the Americans were conducting their Guadalcanal campaign.

America is wonderful,' he said. 'A nice game she plays!'

He was about to close the press conference when Okada asked him what he thought of the campaign in New Guinea.

'A blunder,' Tsuji replied curtly, thrusting the maps and papers on the table into his leather bag. 'Cross the mountains, and you will get the worst of it. Don't you see that? It's as plain as day.'

After the withdrawal from the mountains, the Japanese had found it increasingly hard to reinforce and supply their positions on the New Guinea coast. Time after time, convoys were turned back by Allied air attacks, with such heavy losses that at last Tokyo prohibited supply by ship. With Allied control of the air, supply by airdrop, inadequate in any case, became too costly. At Christmas the Japanese were using a submarine to bring rations to the Buna coast, but submarines were few and too vulnerable to the P.T. boats that were swarming offshore. Barges might have helped, but barge crews had been drawn off to Guadalcanal.

Supply strangulation caused the defeat at Buna, in the opinion of Major Mitsuo Koiwai, the only field grade officer of the South Seas Detachment known to go through the campaign and survive. He had landed near Gona on August 16, fought in the mountains and on the coast, and at the end made his way to safety, infiltrating through the Australian lines with the 150 men left of his battalion. He had then been invalided out of the service with a severe case of malaria. Interrogated in Tokyo at the end of the war, he said, 'We lost Buna because we could not retain air superiority, because we could not supply our troops, and because our navy and air force could not disrupt the enemy supply line.'

This was also the opinion of Colonel J. Sladen Bradley, Chief of Staff of the U.S. 32d Division. In his judgment, 'the successful conclusion of the Buna campaign was brought about by the mere fact that the American and Australian troops were able

171

to "exist" longer than the Japs. That the allied troops took Buna as a result of superior leadership, arms, and tactics is sheer fantasy. Attrition worked both ways, but our supply (although meager) was better than the Jap's supply as they were completely isolated. We lived the longest and therefore took our objective.'

Major Koiwai praised the way the Allies conducted their attack, especially the co-ordination of their advance with their firepower. 'However we were in such a position at Buna that we wondered whether the Americans would bypass us and leave us to starve.'

The Japanese might have been safely bypassed beginning December 20, after they had been confined in two pockets, one at Buna Station, the other at Sanananda, their supplies cut off. Their condition was known to the Allies. In an appreciation of the situation written at the time, General Herring noted that

> Enemy is reduced in numbers, short of ammunition, food and supplies, whilst our Air Force and P.T. boats are preventing any large reinforcements or delivery of supplies. He is weak in artillery, has no tanks and has suffered a series of defeats. He has been attacked by air Force and artillery and has no adequate counter-measures . . .

By December 20 the Allies' main objective, an airfield on the Buna coast, had been achieved at Dobodura. Without much interference from the Japanese, transport planes were bringing in supplies and evacuating the sick and wounded, and airstrips were serving as emergency operating fields for fighters and bombers attacking Rabaul. 'We have practically unchallenged air superiority,' said General Herring; and at sea, P.T. boats were 'effectively protecting' Allied convoys, enabling them to land supplies close to the front.

Strategically, in terms of the return to the Philippines, little would have been lost by leaving the Japanese to starve. Six months were to pass, after Buna, before the Allies were able to resume the advance up the coast of New Guinea.

Disregarding these considerations, General MacArthur and the Australian generals were determined in late December to press for an all-out victory and 'sweep a way clear to the sea'. At Christmas, MacArthur was pressuring General Eichelberger to throw everything into the battle for Buna, using the threat that the Japanese might soon be reinforced, possibly by troops withdrawn from Guadalcanal – if 'results are not achieved shortly the whole picture may radically change'.

MacArthur, with his reputation at stake, had to have a clear-cut victory. In the light of the disaster in the Philippines, he could not afford even the appearance of defeat. And at the end, as his Intelligence Officer, Major General Charles A. Willoughby, has admitted, the battle became a race between MacArthur and the commander at Guadalcanal 'to see who would turn in the first important "land" victory over the Japanese'.

A heavy price was paid for the all-out victory. From their bunkers on the New Guinea coast the Japanese between mid-November and January 22 cost the Allies 6,410 ground troops killed, wounded, and missing, a large proportion of the total battle casualties (beginning July 22) of 8,546. The long-drawn-out struggle for Sanananda became, in the words of the official Australian history, 'a ghastly nightmare'.

> The primaeval swamps, the dank and silent bush, the heavy loss of life, the fixity of purpose of the Japanese, for most of whom death could be the only ending, all combined to make the struggle so appalling that most of the hardened soldiers who were to emerge from it would remember it unwillingly as their most exacting experience of the whole war.

In retrospect, a great deal of the bloodshed appears to have been unnecessary. If it served any purpose, it was an object lesson. General MacArthur, having achieved his victory, was resolved never again to force 'a head-on collision of the bloody, grinding type'. His next objective, Rabaul, was isloated and bypassed; and bypassing was to be his policy wherever possible for the rest of the war. He decreed, 'No more Bunas'.

On the coast of New Guinea, few traces remain of the bloody battle for Buna. In the jungle, vines grow over rusting tanks. Spears of kunai grass hide a commemorative stone bearing Japanese characters. Where Buna Government Station once stood, there stands a peaceful native village of thatched-roofed huts bordered by red and yellow crotons. In the green waters of Entrance Creek lagoon, native children swim, climbing out on the sandspit to watch the mission boat sail by in the empty sea.

At Gona Mission, schoolhouse and towered, reed-and-sago-palm church stand peacefully in the shade of tall tulip trees. Within the church the high altar holds the ashes of Father Benson. All the buildings at Gona were erected, and all the trees planted, after the war. Nothing survived the holocaust in 1942 except a tall wooden cross, scarred by gunfire.

On the beach where gray sands glitter in the sun the eye is drawn to the coral islands on the east and the reef running to the west and to the horizon beyond, the line between pale sea and pale sky from which on a fateful afternoon in July 1942 Japanese warships bore down on the Buna coast.

DOCUMENTATION BY CHAPTER

Chapter I. 'I CAME THROUGH AND I SHALL RETURN'

Pages 13–14
MacArthur's reception in Melbourne has been described in detail by an American newspaperman on the scene, Lewis B. Sebring, Jr, of the New York *Herald Tribune*, in a manuscript lent the author by Hanson W. Baldwin. Hereafter it will be cited as Serbing MS.

Pages 14–15
For the situation in Australia, see George H. Johnston, *Pacific Partner* (N.Y.: 1944), pp. 77–79.

Page 14
'his inimitable strolling magnificence.' E. J. Kahn, Jr, *G.I. Jungle* (Simon & Schuster, N.Y.: 1943), p. 48.

Pages 15–16
The account of MacArthur's landing at Darwin and his journey to Melbourne has been taken from two sources: Frazier Hunt, *The Untold Story of Douglas MacArthur* (N.Y.: 1954), pp. 271–72; and Major General Charles A. Willoughby and John Chamberlain, *MacArthur 1941–1951* (McGraw-Hill, N.Y.: 1954), pp. 61–64.

Page 15
For the situation in the air, see Wesley F. Craven and James L. Cate, eds, *Early Planning and Operations, January 1939 to August 1942* (*The Army Air Forces in World War II*, Vol. I, Chicago; 1948).

Page 16
MacArthur weary and drawn. Lieutenant General George H. Brett, 'The MacArthur I Knew,' *True*, Vol. 21 (Oct. 1947), p. 141.

Page 16
'the Bataan gang.' D. Clayton James, *The Years of MacArthur*, Vol. I, 1880–1941 (Houghton Mifflin, Boston: 1970), p. 569.
Sutherland recommended as successor. Louis Morton, *The Fall of the Philippines* (*U.S. Army in World War II*: 1953), p. 291.
Sutherland 'a hard man.' Willoughby and Chamberlain, *MacArthur 1941–1951*, p. 35.

Page 17
MacArthur an easy motorist to spot. Kahn, *G.I. Jungle*, p. 48.

Page 19
Buna-Gona considered a major threat. George H. Johnston, *The Toughest Fighting in the World* (Duell, Sloan and Pearce, N.Y.: 1943), p. 106.

Page 19
'we saw one another's tears.' Willoughby and Chamberlain, *MacArthur 1941–1951*, p. 15.

Pages 22–24
Sebring MS.

Chapter II.   THE JAPANESE INVASION
In addition to military details by McCarthy and Milner, this chapter is based on James Benson, *Prisoner's Base and Home Again* (Robert Hale, Ltd, London: 1957).

Pages 25–26
The afternoon of 21 July at Gona and the evening of 20 July. Preface by Father James Benson (quoting ltr, May Hayman 'to her people at Canberra,' 5 Aug. 42) to Seizo Okada, MS, 'Lost Troops', Australian War Memorial, Canberra.

Page 26
'Father! Father! Come quickly . . . ' Benson, preface to 'Lost Troops'.

Page 28
'dark, uncivilized place.' Lieutenant General Tsutomu Yoshihara, *Southern Cross, An Account of the Eastern New Guinea Campaign* (Tokyo: 1955), translation by Doris Heath in Australian War Memorial.

Page 29
Children's exercise books and the military police. Father Benson's notes on 'Lost Troops'.
The Japanese landings at Buna. Japanese Monograph No. 96, United States Army Center of Military History (C.M.H.).

Pages 29–30
Australian military actions along the track and at Kokoda. Raymond Paull, *Retreat from Kokoda* (Heinemann, Melbourne, London, Toronto: 1958), pp. 42–68.

Pages 31–32
Vernon's activities and quote, 'The thick white mist . . .' Report by Dr Vernon in A.N.G.A.U. War Diary, quoted in McCarthy, p. 129. Also see Captain G. H. Vernon, MS, 'A War Diary, The Owen Stanley Campaign, July–November 1942, Australian War Memorial.

Page 34
Figures on the landings in the Buna-Gona area. Official Japanese naval account, Japanese Invasion Eastern New Guinea, quoted in Milner, p. 70.

Page 35
Capture and death of Sisters Hayman and Parkinson. Father Benson, preface to 'Lost Troops'.

Chapter III.   MILNE BAY: NIGHT BATTLES IN THE RAIN
In addition to McCarthy and Milner, general sources are Douglas Gillison, *Royal Australian Air Force, 1939–42* (Australian War Memorial series, *Australia in the War of 1939–1945*) and *Samuel Milner*, 'The Battle of Milne Bay,' *Military Review*, Vol. XXX (April 1950).

Page 38
'tired, drawn, and nervous.' George C. Kenney, *General Kenney Reports* (Duell, Sloan and Pearce, N.Y.: 1949), p. 31.
'raked his spirit raw.' Brett, 'The MacArthur I Knew,' p. 143.
MacArthur's reply to Marshall, 2 Aug. 42, is partially quoted in McCarthy, p. 121 and abstracted in Milner, pp. 72–73.

Page 39
'I don't think . . . than this.' Paull, *Retreat from Kokoda*, p. 104.

Page 39
'literally come to a standstill.' Honner, in McCarthy, p. 142.

Page 43
'Who goes...morning!' H.Q. 7 Aus. Inf. Bde. Sept. 42, Lessons from Recent Fighting, p. 2, copy in Milner File.

Page 44
'put everything in.' McCarthy, p. 176.

Page 46
'take immediate stations.' Clowes, Rpt. by Comd. Milne Force on Opns. 25 Aug.-2 Sept. 42, p. 4, Milner File.

Page 47
365 sick and 164 wounded. Allan S. Walker, *The Island Campaigns* (Australian War Memorial series, *Australia in the War of 1939–45:* 1957), p. 57.

Page 47
Chinese crew of the *Anshun.* Interv by author with Don McBeath, passenger on the *Anshun,* 13 Nov. 67.
Casualty figures from Clowes Rpt.; McCarthy, p. 185; Milner, p. 87.
First repulse of Japanese amphibious operation. Samuel Eliot Morrison, *Breaking the Bismarck's Barrier (History of the United States Naval Operations in World War II, Vol. VI:* 1950), p. 39.

Page 47
Slim quote from McCarthy, p. 187, fn. 5.

Page 48
Comment 'ungenerous.' McCarthy, p. 186.

Chapter IV.   RETREAT FROM ISURAVA
This chapter relies, in addition to McCarthy, primarily on Paull, *Retreat from Kokoda.*

Page 49
Australia's Thermopylae. Lieutenant Colonel R. Honner, 'The 39th at Isurava,' *Stand-To,* July–Aug. 1956, p. 9.
shirts and shorts . . . green. William B. Russell, *The Second Fourteenth Battalion* (Angus & Robertson, Sydney & London: 1948), p. 123.

Page 49
Honner felt the line would hold. Honner, 'The 39th at Isurava,' p. 12.

Page 50
'Honner was the coolest man . . . ' McCarthy, p. 203, fn. 9.

Page 51
'an emaciated skeleton.' Benson, *Prisoner's Base and Home Again* (paperback edition, 1959) p. 59.

Pages 53–54
All night . . . spanning rushing waters. Osmar White, *Green Armor* (Norton, N.Y.: 1945), pp. 193–203.

Page 54
Osmar White returned with deep misgivings. *Ibid.*, p. 201.

Page 59
Their faces had a waxy pallor. Russell, *The Second Fourteenth Battalion*, p. 173.

Chapter V. 'MUST I ALWAYS LEAD A FORLORN HOPE?'

Pages 61–62
He left the choice . . . from the 32d Division. Milner, pp. 91–92.

Page 63
When they disembarked . . . ten feet away. E. J. Kahn, Jr., 'The Terrible Days of Company E,' *The Saturday Evening Post*, 8 Jan. 44, p. 11.

Pages 63–64
That evening General MacArthur . . . unfavorable. McCarthy, p. 235.

Page 64
'Must I always . . . quick conquest.' Willoughby and Chamberlain, *MacArthur 1941–1951*, pp. 84, 83.

Page 64
'energize the situation.' McCarthy, p. 235.

Page 64
The division's 128th . . . Seven Mile Airdrome. A/A Rpt. 128th Inf. Regt., 17 Sept. 42–15 Mar. 43, Washington National Records Center (W.R.N.C.), General Archives Division, Washington, D.C. 2049.
'Dimple-knees.' Sebring MS.

Page 65
He considered MacArthur's 'flank operation' unsound. Foreword by Lieutenant General Sir Sydney Rowell to Paull, *Retreat from Kokoda*, p. xvii.

Page 65
a landing field . . . to General MacArthur. Kenney. *General Kenney Reports*, pp. 41–42; 91.

Page 65
'small and quiet man' McCarthy, p. 73.

Page 66
a cane chair . . . white gloves. Dispatch by Byron Darnton to New York *Times*, 7 Oct. 42.

Pages 66–67
It was true . . . Headquarters in Tokyo. Seizo Okada, 'Lost Troops.'

Pages 67–68
The Japanese planning staffs . . . 'and hold the airfield.' Paull, *Retreat from Kokoda*, pp. 268–69.

Page 68
All night . . . mountains had begun. Okada, 'Lost Troops.'

Page 68
General Blamey reported . . . Paull, *Retreat from Kokoda*, p. 271.

Page 69
'like a bloody barometer.' McCarthy, p. 225.
On 1 October . . . take Buna. G.H.Q. S.W.P.A., Operation Instruction No. 19, 1 Oct. 42, W.N.R.C.

Chapter VI.   THE AMERICAN ADVANCE BY MOUNTAIN AND SEA

Pages 70–72
Sebring MS. On the war correspondents, see Pat Robinson, *The Fight for New Guinea* (Random House, N.Y.: 1943); Geoffrey Reading, *Papuan Story* (Angus & Robertson, Sydney & London: 1946); George H. Johnston, *New Guinea Diary* (Victor Gollancz, Ltd., London: 1944).

Page 72
'Lloyd . . . don't stop.' McCarthy, p. 280.

Pages 72–76
Kahn, 'The Terrible Days of Company E,' and Hanson W. Baldwin, 'Doughboys' March a High Point in War,' N. Y. *Times*, 7 May 1944.

Page 73
Leeches . . . Jap patrol. Milner, p. 112.

Pages 75–76
It was one green hell . . . 'will it never end?' Milner, pp.
114–15.

Pages 78–80
Memo, Captain Maxwell Emerson for CG 32d Infantry Div.,
27 Mar. 43, sub: Activities of the 107th Quartermaster Detach-
ment at Oro Bay and Hariko, New Guinea, W.N.R.C.; ltr.,
Lieutenant Colonel Laurence A. McKenny to General Mac-
Nider, n.d., sub: Report of Attack by unidentified bomber . . .
18 Oct. 42, and other documents in 32d Div. G-3 Rpt.,
WNRC.

Page 81
'NOT satisfactory.' McCarthy, p. 290.

Chapter VII.   HORII'S FIGHTING WITHDRAWAL
Details not specifically cited are from McCarthy, also Paull,
Retreat from Kokoda.

Page 83
cooking pots were still warm. Captain H. G. McCammon and
Captain C. H. Hodge, 'The Kokoda Trail,' *Nulli Secundus Log*
(pub. by 2/2nd Infantry Battalion, Sydney: 1946), p. 88.

Page 86
The time and place of Horii's death, of which several conflict-
ing accounts exist, are taken from Milner, who cited Japanese
documents, p. 143, fn. 47 and p. 213, fn. 1. For New Guinea
rivers 'unbelievably rapid,' Yoshihara, *Southern Cross.* The
story of the rescue attempt, including Horii's and Tanaka's
last words, was brought to Japanese headquarters by one of
their orderlies, who swam the Kumusi at its mouth and made
his way to the Buna coast. Okada, 'Lost Troops.'

Pages 86–87
Okada, 'Lost Troops.'

Page 87
Looking up . . . from the decks above. Benson, *Prisoner's Base
and Home Again*, p. 65.
jungle fighters from Formosa. Yoshihara, *Southern Cross.*

Chapter VIII.   THE ALLIES' OFFENSIVE BEGINS – AND
STALLS
The air war in the Buna campaign has been covered in Wesley
F. Craven and James L. Cate, eds., *The Pacific: Guadalcanal
to Saipan, August 1942 to July 1944* (*The Army Air Forces in
World War II*, Vol. IV, Chicago: 1950).

Page 89
The general flew . . . in the corner. Sebring MS.

Page 90
Belief that the order was political. Milner, p. 138.

Page 90
General Kenney . . . coastal plain. Kenney, *General Kenney Reports*, pp. 137–38.

Page 91
General Blamey . . . at once. McCarthy, p. 385.

Page 92
'like the eve of a celebration.' Ltr., Colonel John E. Harbert to author, 26 Oct. 64.

Page 93
'The artillery in this theater flies.' Ltr., Kenney to Lieutenant General H. H. Arnold, 24 Oct. 42, quoted in Milner, p. 135.

Pages 93–98
In a daring commando . . . medical supplies. Lida Mayo, MS, 'The Small Ships of General MacArthur,' based on Harding's diary, correspondence with participants, official documents, Geoffrey Reading, *Papuan Story*, and John W. O'Brien, *Guns and Gunners* (Angus & Robertson, Sydney & London: 1950).

Chapter IX. 'TAKE BUNA'

Page 101
MacArthur's communiqué of November 20 and message of November 21 to Harding. Sebring MS.
'regardless of losses.' McCarthy, p. 359.
'hand-to-mouth . . . basis.' Ltr., Harding to Herring, 28 Nov. 42, quoted in Milner, p. 199.

Page 104
fresh and healthy . . . plenty of cigarettes. McCammon and Hodge, 'The Kokoda Trail,' p. 92.
'to clean things . . . Japs right out.' McCarthy, pp. 394–95.

Page 104
General Kenney admitted . . . got ashore. Kenney, *General Kenney Reports*, p. 147.
'a bitter pill . . . to swallow.' *Ibid.*, p. 151.

Page 105
General Kenney . . . get them moving. *Ibid.*, pp. 150–51.

Page 106
'Many more failed than succeeded.' Ltr., Colonel Herbert A. Smith to Samuel Milner, 20 Jan. 50, Milner, p. 197.

Page 106
'somewhat conspicuous.' Kahn, *G.I. Jungle*, p. 93.
a guard 'commendably imperturbable.' Entry for 26 Nov. 42 in Harding's Diary, with notation, 'Written by E. J. Kahn, Jr.'

Page 107
'The long march home' . . . weak coffee. *Ibid.*, and Sebring MS.
'an air of rustic tranquillity.' Harding Diary, 27 Nov. 42.

Pages 107–108
Three days . . . in a river. *Ibid.*, 29 Nov. 42.

Page 108
a plane landed . . . at Dobodura the following morning. McCarthy, p. 372.

Page 108
Larr's very adverse report. As Larr's report is not included in GHQ G-3 files, it was probably made orally (Larr was killed in a plane crash in 1947), Milner, p. 202, fn. 23. Its gist is in Colonel Knight's Buna Report, pp. 16, 21 (copy in Milner File) and *General Kenney Reports*, p. 154.

Pages 109–110
Conversation between Sutherland and Harding. Milner, pp. 202–03.

Page 110
recommendation . . . open to question. Milner, p. 203, citing interview Louis Morton with Sutherland, 12 Nov. 46.

Pages 110–111
General Eichelberger flew . . . Buna front in the morning. Robert L. Eichelberger, *Our Jungle Road to Tokyo* (Viking, N.Y.: 1950), p. 21; Milner, p. 204, citing interviews with Eichelberger and Byers 1 June 50.

Page 111
Before noon . . . in the Japanese perimeter. Harding Diary, 1 Dec. 42.

Chapter X.   THE FIRST BREAKTHROUGH IN THE JAPANESE DEFENSES

Pages 112–113
Narrative of Lieutenant Robert H. Odell, Dec. 42, 12th Sta.
Hosp., Australia, Milner File.

Page 113
Colonel Mott . . . that very night. Harding Diary, 30 Nov.,
1 Dec.

Page 114
There was one dash . . . Station. Milner, p. 205.

Page 114
Around midnight . . . counterattack. Memorandum, Colonel
John W. Mott, 10 Dec. 42, Milner File; Harding Diary, 2 Dec.

Page 114
'bearded . . . Potomac.' Harding Diary, 2 Dec.

Page 114
Sometime . . . had been none. Ltr., Smith to Milner, 16 Mar. 50,
Milner File.

Page 115
Suspecting . . . had not fought. Eichelberger, *Our Jungle Road
to Tokyo*, p. 25.

Page 115
At this point . . . to the ground. Mott Memo; Harding Diary,
2 Dec.; Memo, Mott for General MacArthur, 7 Dec. 42, Milner
File.
Major Smith . . . pressure himself. Ltr., Smith to Milner, 16
Mar. 50.

Page 116
Twenty-four hours . . . succeeded. Ltrs, General Martin to
General Ward, 1, 6 Mar. 51, quoted in Milner, pp. 210, 235.
Eichelberger . . . conduct in battle. Eichelberger to General
Sutherland, 6 Dec. 42, quoted in Milner, p. 245.

Page 117
Early that afternoon . . . 'Harding hasn't failed.' Sebring MS.

Page 117
That evening . . . in Port Moresby. Harding Diary 3–5 Dec.

Page 118
'sunk to zero.' Ltr of 4 Dec., quoted in McCarthy, p. 450.
'a doughboy . . . War.' Ltr, Eichelberger to Sutherland 4 Dec.

Page 119
'simply collapsed . . . foot.' Odell Narrative.
'a terrible experience.' Grose Diary, 3 Dec., Milner File.

Japanese were 'not in great force'. Eichelberger to Sutherland,
4 Dec.

Page 120
He was Staff Sergeant . . . Village. Ltr, Colonel Gordon B.
Rogers to Milner, 26 June 50, Milner File. Other details on
Bottcher are in Eichelberger, *Our Jungle Road to Tokyo*, p. 32.

Page 120
Early in the afternoon . . . half the men. Odell Narrative.

Pages 120–121
Behind Odell's men . . . jeep. Eichelberger, *Our Jungle Road to
Tokyo*, pp. 30–31.

Page 121
Reporting this breakthrough . . . 'on your fingers'. Eichelberger
to Sutherland, 5 Dec.

Page 122
Elated . . . 'pants!' Eichelberger, *Our Jungle Road to Tokyo*, p.
32. Obviously ignorant of the diarrhea on the 'Ghost Mountain'
climb, Eichelberger thought the pants had been rotted by
swamp water. *Ibid.*

Pages 122–123
On the gray sands . . . no more attacks occurred. Odell Narrative.

Page 123
Bottcher . . . 'even known'. Eichelberger, *Our Jungle Road to
Tokyo*, p. 32.

Chapter XI.   THE AUSTRALIANS TAKE GONA
This chapter is based mainly on McCarthy.

Page 128
All the attackers . . . 'no easy nut to crack'. Honner, This is the
39th', p. 221.

Page 130
'Gona's gone!' *Ibid.*, p. 223.

Page 130
On the parapets . . . gas masks. Paull, *Retreat from Kokoda*, p. 295.
'waving a samurai sword and roaring like a bull.' Honner, 'This is the 39th', p. 224.

Page 130
The most important lesson of Gona. Paull, *Retreat from Kokoda*, p. 297.

Chapter XII.   THE IMPATIENCE OF THE GENERALS

Page 133
'we must go forward yard by yard.' Ltr, Eichelberger to Sutherland, 11 Dec., Milner File.

Pages 133–136
For Japanese details including the flight to Rabaul, Yoshihara, *Southern Cross.* Yoshihara was in the party.

Page 133
Japanese strategy and preparations 'presumably against Port Moresby'. Louis Morton, *Strategy and Command: The First Two Years (U.S. Army in W.W. II:* 1962), pp. 364–67.

Page 136
The escape . . . wearing thin. Ltr, MacArthur to Eichelberger, 13 Dec., Milner File.
'did not want to get the Chief's hopes up.' Ltr, Eichelberger to Sutherland, 13–14 Dec. Milner File.

Page 139
The Australian infantrymen . . . like gay cockades. F. Tillman Durdin, dispatch in N.Y. *Times*, 21 Dec. 42.
In the dash . . . beyond Cape Endaiadere. Rpt of Opns, Aus. Inf. Brigade Grp. at Cape Endaiadere, copy in Milner File.

Page 140
And yet . . . far from over. Durdin in N.Y. *Times*, 21 Dec. 42.

Chapter XIII.   PUSHING ON TO VICTORY AT BUNA

Pages 141–143
For Wootten's advance see McCarthy, pp. 465–70.

Page 144
the general, 'most impatient', had refused. Grose Diary, 21 Dec.
'Captain Meyer . . . that is an order.' Ltr, Meyer to Milner, 13 Mar. 51. Milner File.

Page 145
'troops in their first fight . . . in the dark.' Ltr, Eichelberger to Sutherland, 22 Dec., Milner File.
'I think we are going places.' Ltr of 24 Dec., Milner File.

Page 146
'all time low.' Ltr of 25 Dec., Milner File.

Page 146
staff officers advised . . . in his life. *Ibid.*
close to being relieved. Grose Comments on Milner MS., Milner File.

Page 146
Eichelberger's Christmas dinner . . . more progress. Ltrs, Eichelberger to MacArthur 25 and 26 Dec., Milner File; *Our Jungle Road to Tokyo*, p. 47.

Pages 147–747
'Where you have a company . . . radically change.' Ltr, MacArthur to Eichelberger, 25 Dec., Milner File.

Page 147
all the fighting strength . . . 'noses at you'. Ltrs, Eichelberger to MacArthur 25 and 26 Dec.
'Don't we have any tanks in this area?' Sugiyama Diaries, entry for 9 Jan. 43, copy lent the author by John Toland.
'The big shots . . . might understand!' John Toland, *The Rising Sun* (Random House, N.Y.: 1970), p. 425.
On Christmas night . . . the coast. Milner, p. 314, fn. 28.

Page 147
The Japanese . . . first priority. Yoshihara, *Southern Cross*.

Pages 147–148
Before leaving Tokyo . . . 'taking away the ladder'. John Toland, *The Rising Sun*, pp. 418–19; 425.

Page 148
The barge project . . . way to Sanananda. Yoshihara, *Southern Cross*; Milner, p. 315, citing Buna Shitai Opns. Orders, 27 and 31 Dec. 42.

Page 149
General Eichelberger . . . 'on to victory'. Eichelberger to Sutherland, 27 Dec., Milner File.

Page 149
Late that night . . . 'fears of darkness'. Eichelberger, *Our Jungle Road to Tokyo*, p. 48.

Pages 149–150
Even better . . . to the Urbana front. Milner, p. 329.

Pages 150–151
Eichelberger took Sutherland . . . 'to being relieved'. Milner, pp. 309–11; intervs, Milner with Grose, 15 Nov. 50 and 1 Feb. 51, Milner File.

Page 151
'famous "Triangle" . . . taken,' Ltr, Eichelberger to Colonel Rex Chandler, DC/S I Corps, Rockhamton, 31 Dec. 42, quoted in Milner, p. 315.

Pages 151–152
Eichelberger was . . . Blamey. Ltr, Major General Jens A. Doe to General Ward, 3 Mar. 51, Milner File; ltr, Colonel Charles A. Dawley to General Ward, 7 Mar. 51, cited by Milner, p. 330.

Page 152
General Herring rubbed . . . offensive on Giropa. Two ltrs from Eichelberger to Sutherland, 30 Dec. 42, one dated 10 a.m., the other written in the evening, Milner File.

Page 152
The attack was . . . no more than ankle deep. 'Operational Observations', in Rpt of Inspection of Buna-Dobodura by Colonel Sverdrup, 5 Jan. 43, A.F.P.A.C. Engr File, copy, Milner File.

Page 153
Colonel Grose, standing . . . the next three days. Grose Comments on Milner MS and ltr, Grose to General Ward, 26 Feb. 51, quoted in Milner, p. 313.

Page 153
The best he could promise . . . on the Warren front. Ltr, Eichelberger to Sutherland, 31 Dec., Milner File.
'Everybody's spirits . . . old-time flourish.' Ltrs, MacNab to Milner 25 Nov. 49 and 18 Apr. 50, Milner File.

Pages 154–155
That day . . . Japanese account. Yoshihara, *Southern Cross.*

Page 155
As Arnold's tanks . . . hanging from a tree. McCarthy, pp. 484–85.

Page 155
Eventually 1,400 . . . 132 missing. Milner, p. 323, cited 32d Division and 18th Aust. Inf. Brigade figures as of 6 Jan. 43.

Pages 155–156
On Sunday . . . bony. Durdin dispatch of 3 Jan. in N.Y. *Times* of 8 Jan. 43.

Page 156
'Is your secretary sick?' Ltr, Eichelberger to Sutherland, 6 Jan. 43, Milner File.
On January 9 . . . MacArthur, copy of ltr in Milner File.
MacArthur's communiqué of January 8 and Order of the Day on January 9. *The Reports of General MacArthur*, Vol. I (Tokyo: 1950), pp. 98–99.

Page 157
The triumphant . . . 'and mine'. Eichelberger, *Our Jungle Road to Tokyo*, p. 57.

Chapter XIV. THE END AT SANANANDA

Page 158
Early on Christmas . . . saddles. Reverend F. J. Hartley, *Sanananda Interlude* (1949), quoted in McCarthy, p. 507.

Page 159
'red-raw . . . in bandages instead of boots.' Honner, 'This is the 39th', p. 229.

Page 159
welcomed there by General Eichelberger . . . 'my eyes were wet.' Eichelberger, *Our Jungle Road to Tokyo*, pp. 56–57, ltr, Eichelberger to MacArthur, 14 Jan. 43.

Page 161
On the last day of December . . . Dampier Strait. Yoshihara, *Southern Cross*.

Page 162
Buoyed by hope . . . *I Am Troubled*. Wada's Diary, 18 Dec. 42–18 Jan. 43, is quoted in full in Paull, *Retreat from Kokoda*, pp. 298–305. Wada came to New Guinea with the 3d Bn, 144th Infantry. Milner, p. 213, fn. 40.

Page 162
On January 12 . . . moon was favorable. Rad., General Oda to CofS, 18th Army, 12 Jan. 43, and 18th Army Opns Orders M.O. No. A-72, 13 Jan. 43, quoted in Milner, pp. 347–48.

Page 165
They found . . . splintered palm trees. Photograph by Allied Air Forces, in McCarthy between pp. 514–15.
'mud, filth and death.' McCarthy, p. 522.

Page 165

The withdrawal of the sick . . . those able to walk. Yoshihara, *Southern Cross*.

Watching the boats . . . by shellfire. Paull, *Retreat from Kokoda*, pp. 298, 305.

Page 166

When the last unit . . . shot themselves. Yoshiharar, *Southern Cross*.

Page 166

The heavy rains . . . across the western sky. Sergeant Richardson, *Yank* staff correspondent, quoted in William F. McCartney, *The Jungleers: A History of the 41st Infantry Division* (Infantry Journal Press, Washington, D.C.: 1948), p. 203.

Chapter XV. 'NO MORE BUNAS'

Page 167

'A striking victory.' Order of the Day, General Herring, facsimile in Milner, p. 365.

'annihilated.' *The Reports of General MacArthur*, Vol. I, p. 198.

At Guadalcanal . . . 4,245 were wounded. John Miller, Jr, *Guadalcanal. The First Offensive (U.S. Army in W.W. II: 1949)*, p. 350.

marching to Dobodura . . . 'under the tropic sun'. Honner, 'This is the 39th', p. 230.

Pages 167–168

Twenty years . . . of the war. Ltr, Colonel John E. Harbert to author, 26 Oct. 64.

George H. Johnston's book on Buna is entitled *The Toughest Fighting in the World* (Duell, Sloan and Pearce, N.Y.: 1943).

'certainly the nastiest' of the war. Samuel Eliot Morison, *Breaking the Bismarcks Barrier*, p. 45, fn. 3.

Page 168

'Lack of planning . . . Japanese.' Sebring MS, quoting interview with White.

The Japanese planners . . . rice. John Vader, *New Guinea: the tide is stemmed* (Ballantine Books, N.Y.: 1971), p. 14.

Page 169

'a poor man's war.' Eichelberger, *Our Jungle Road to Tokyo*, p. 61.

Page 169
'a repetition of Pershing's attitude.' Brett, 'The MacArthur I Knew', p. 147.
'had little to do with soldiers.' *Ibid.*

Page 170
'to have developed the mantle . . . Japanese privates.' Vader, *New Guinea: the tide is stemmed*, p. 62.

Page 170
Between July . . . 'magnificent tragedy'. Yoshihara, *Southern Cross*.

Pages 170–171
Japanese war correspondent . . . 'as plain as day.' Seizo Okada, 'Lost Troops'; and on Tsuji see Toland, *Rising Sun*, p. 157.

Page 171
'We lost . . . supply line.' Milner, p. 374.

Pages 171–172
'the successful conclusion . . . our objective.' Ltr, Bradley to Milner, 26 Jan. 50, Milner File.
'However we . . . to starve.' Milner, p. 374.
Enemy is reduced . . . countermeasures . . . McCarthy, p. 510.

Page 172
'We have . . . effectively protecting.' *Ibid.*
'sweep a way clear to the sea.' McCarthy, p. 508.

Page 173
'to see who . . . the Japanese.' Willoughby and Chamberlain, *MacArthur 1941–1951*, p. 92.

Page 173
'a ghastly nightmare . . . the whole war.' McCarthy, p. 508.
'a head-on collision of the bloody, grinding type.' Willoughby and Chamberlain, *MacArthur 1941–1951*, p. 100.
'No more Bunas.' *Ibid.*, p. 92.

Pages 173–174
On the coast . . . Buna coast. Notes by the author on visit to Buna Coast in November 1967.

NEL BESTSELLERS

Crime			
T031 306	UNPLEASANTNESS AT THE BELLONA CLUB		
		Dorothy L. Sayers	85p
T031 373	STRONG POISON	*Dorothy L. Sayers*	80p
T026 663	THE DOCUMENTS IN THE CASE	*Dorothy L. Sayers*	50p
Fiction			
T029 522	HATTERS CASTLE	*A. J. Cronin*	£1.00
T030 199	CRUSADER'S TOMB	*A. J. Cronin*	£1.25
T031 276	THE CITADEL	*A. J. Cronin*	95p
T029 158	THE STARS LOOK DOWN	*A. J. Cronin*	£1.00
T022 021	THREE LOVES	*A. J. Cronin*	90p
T032 523	THE DREAM MERCHANTS	*Harold Robbins*	£1.10
T031 705	THE PIRATE	*Harold Robbins*	£1.00
T033 791	THE CARPETBAGGERS	*Harold Robbins*	£1.25
T031 667	WHERE LOVE HAS GONE	*Harold Robbins*	£1.00
T032 647	THE ADVENTURERS	*Harold Robbins*	£1.25
T031 659	THE INHERITORS	*Harold Robbins*	95p
T031 586	STILETTO	*Harold Robbins*	60p
T033 805	NEVER LEAVE ME	*Harold Robbins*	70p
T032 698	NEVER LOVE A STRANGER	*Harold Robbins*	95p
T032 531	A STONE FOR DANNY FISHER	*Harold Robbins*	90p
T031 659	79 PARK AVENUE	*Harold Robbins*	80p
T032 655	THE BETSY	*Harold Robbins*	95p
T031 594	THE LONELY LADY	*Harold Robbins*	£1.25
T032 639	EVENING IN BYZANTIUM	*Irwin Shaw*	80p
T033 732	RICH MAN, POOR MAN	*Irwin Shaw*	£1.35
Historical			
T023 079	LORD GEOFFREY'S FANCY	*Alfred Duggan*	60p
T024 903	THE KING OF ATHELNEY	*Alfred Duggan*	60p
T032 817	FOX 1: PRESS GANG	*Adam Hardy*	50p
T032 825	FOX 2: PRIZE MONEY	*Adam Hardy*	50p
T032 833	FOX 3: SIEGE	*Adam Hardy*	50p
Science Fiction			
T029 492	STRANGER IN A STRANGE LAND	*Robert Heinlein*	80p
T029 484	I WILL FEAR NO EVIL	*Robert Heinlein*	95p
T031 462	DUNE	*Frank Herbert*	£1.25
T032 671	DUNE MESSIAH	*Frank Herbert*	75p
War			
T027 066	COLDITZ: THE GERMAN STORY	*Reinhold Egger*	50p
T025 438	LILIPUT FLEET	*A. Cecil Hampshire*	50p
T026 299	TRAWLERS GO TO WAR	*Lund & Ludlam*	50p
Western			
T031 284	EDGE 1: THE LONER	*George Gilman*	50p
T032 671	EDGE 2: TEN THOUSAND DOLLARS AMERICAN		
		George Gilman	50p
T024 490	ADAM STEELE 1: THE VIOLENT PEACE	*George Gilman*	35p
General			
T033 155	SEX MANNERS FOR MEN	*Robert Chartham*	60p
T023 206	THE BOOK OF LOVE	*Dr David Delvin*	90p
T028 828	THE LONG BANANA SKIN	*Michael Bentine*	90p

NEL P.O. BOX 11, FALMOUTH TR10 9EN, CORNWALL:

For U.K.: Customers should include to cover postage, 19p for the first book plus 9p per copy for each additional book ordered up to a maximum charge of 73p.

For B.F.P.O. and Eire: Customers should include to cover postage, 19p for the first book plus 9p per copy for the next 6 and thereafter 3p per book.

For Overseas: Customers should include to cover postage. 20p for the first book plus 10p per copy for each additional book.

Name ....

Address ....

....

Title ....
(MAY)

Whilst every effort is made to maintain prices, new editions or printings may carry an increased price and the actual price of the edition supplied will apply.